M000316577

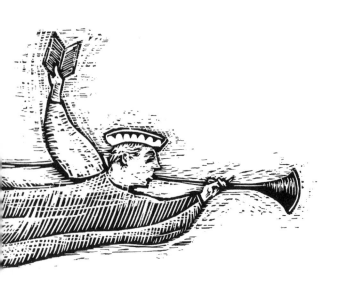

Jacob: *a brief theological introduction*

This publication was made possible by generous support from the Laura F. Willes Center for Book of Mormon Studies, part of the Neal A. Maxwell Institute for Religious Scholarship at Brigham Young University.

Published by the Neal A. Maxwell Institute for Religious Scholarship, Brigham Young University, Provo, Utah. The copyright for the 2013 text of The Book of Mormon is held by The Church of Jesus Christ of Latter-day Saints, Salt Lake City, Utah; that text is quoted throughout and used by permission.

Printed in the United States of America

ISBN: 978-0-8425-0011-1

LIBRARY OF CONGRESS CONTROL NUMBER: 2020902178

Jacob

a brief theological introduction

BRIGHAM YOUNG UNIVERSITY

NEAL A. MAXWELL INSTITUTE

PROVO, UTAH

Deidre Nicole Green

The Book of Mormon: brief theological introductions series seeks Christ in scripture by combining intellectual rigor and the disciple's yearning for holiness. It answers Elder Neal A. Maxwell's call to explore the book's "divine architecture": "There is so much more in the Book of Mormon than we have yet discovered. The book's divine architecture and rich furnishings will increasingly unfold to our view, further qualifying it as '*a marvelous work and a wonder.*' (Isaiah 29:14) . . . All the rooms in this mansion need to be explored, whether by valued traditional scholars or by those at the cutting edge. Each plays a role, and one LDS scholar cannot say to the other, '*I have no need of thee.*'"[1] (1 Corinthians 12:21)

For some time, faithful scholars have explored the book's textual history, reception, historicity, literary quality, and more. This series focuses particularly on theology—the scholarly practice of exploring a scriptural text's implications and its lens on God's work in the world. Series volumes invite Latter-day Saints to discover additional dimensions of this treasured text but leave to prophets and apostles their unique role of declaring its definitive official doctrines. In this case, theology, as opposed to authoritative doctrine, relates to the original sense of the term as, literally, reasoned "God talk." The word also designates a well-developed academic field, but it is the more general sense of the term that most often applies here. By engaging each scriptural book's theology on its own terms, this series explores the spiritual and intellectual force of the ideas appearing in the Latter-day Saints' "keystone" scripture.

Series authors and editors possess specialized professional training that informs their work but, significantly, each takes Christ as theology's proper end because he is the proper end of all scripture and all reflection on it. We, too, "talk of Christ, we rejoice in Christ, we preach of Christ...that our children may know to what source they may look for a remission of their sins" (2 Nephi 25:26). Moreover, while experts in the modern disciplines of philosophy, theology, literature, and history, series authors and editors also work explicitly within the context of personal and institutional commitments both to Christian discipleship and to The Church of Jesus Christ of Latter-day Saints. These volumes are not official Church publications but can be best understood in light of these deep commitments. And because we acknowledge that scripture demands far more than intellectual experimentation, we call readers' attention to the processes of conversion and sanctification at play on virtually every scriptural page.

Individual series authors offer unique approaches but, taken together, they model a joint invitation to readers to engage scripture in their own way. No single approach to theology or scriptural interpretation commands pre-eminence in these volumes. No volume pretends to be the final word on theological reflection for its part of the Book of Mormon. Varied perspectives and methodologies are evident throughout. This is intentional. In addition, though we recognize love for the Book of Mormon is a "given" for most Latter–day Saint readers, we also share the conviction that, like the gospel of Jesus Christ itself, the Book of Mormon is inexhaustible.[2] These volumes invite readers to slow down and read scripture more thoughtfully and transformatively. Elder Maxwell cautioned against reading the Book of Mormon as "hurried tourists" who scarcely venture beyond "the entry hall."[3] To that end, we dedicate this series to his apostolic conviction that there is always more to learn from the Book of Mormon and much to be gained from our faithful search for Christ in its pages.

—The Editors

Contents

Introduction

Jacob has a unique voice in the Book of Mormon; his particular history and experience shape a rare and distinct perspective among the various authors of the text. A vulnerable and empathic religious leader, Jacob concerns himself largely with issues of social justice, demonstrating that religious life and social life should not be separated into distinct spheres. Jacob's personal experience of suffering, his compassion for those on the margins of society, his concern for equality, and his commitment to forming a faithful and just community inform his testimony of Jesus Christ in a way that highlights many of the salient issues of the twenty-first century. Reading the Book of Mormon through the lens of the book of Jacob can equip readers to see more clearly the entire Book of Mormon's relevance in these latter days.

In a single verse, Jacob implores the Nephite men of his time, as well as contemporary readers, to "hearken" to his words, to "arouse the faculties of your souls," and to "shake yourselves that ye may awake from the slumber of death; and loose yourselves from the pains of hell" (Jacob 3:11). Because Jacob's ministry is devoted in part to waking people up from the slumber of complacency and inequality, the book named for him fittingly moves in unpredictable and counterintuitive directions, jarring us to revive our spiritual senses and give our attention to the order of creation and the nature of redemption. In his book, Jacob consistently aids us in understanding atonement, often by pointing away from himself and allowing the abject to instruct the privileged on how to live a godly life. For Jacob, redemption and salvation are communal and made possible only in dialogue with others. In both word and deed, Jacob seeks to heal a fractured society.

Jacob demonstrates not only that individuals need redemption, but also that sometimes the church needs to be turned upside down in order to be turned right side up. At the same time, he teaches that the grace of atonement can put the pieces of our lives back together, restoring both the individual self and communities to wholeness and cohesion after they have been fragmented by traumatic suffering or sinful practices. At the book of Jacob, the Book of Mormon takes a sharp turn from the narrative to the normative—from descriptions of one family's sojourn and divine promises to be fulfilled in the future to prescriptions for human behavior to be enacted in the here and now. As scripture, Jacob's exhortations and reprimands stand before us today with no less binding force than they had on the Nephites of his time.

One overarching theme throughout the book of Jacob is equality. Jacob feels a responsibility to dismantle the social hierarchies that the Nephites have constructed. Jacob razes these false hierarchies by deconstructing the false theological views that undergird them. His profound understanding of the fact that all people are inherently equal informs every aspect of his ministry. He continually emphasizes God's universal love for humanity as the means by which we can learn to love ourselves and others. If God sees all of us as equals, we should see each other as equals. In other words, we can develop charity only as we recognize our fundamental equality. Because the recognition of equality requires humility, Jacob skillfully employs those members of society that we might, in our prideful way, consider to be less than us spiritually in order to teach us spiritual truths.

A second important theme is relationship. As human beings we are connected to each other, and God and Christ are always seeking to become more connected with us. Jacob shows us that our religious lives and our social lives are inseparably intertwined, and this interconnectedness has concrete and material implications for the commandment to love our neighbor. He teaches that the sins of individuals can have serious consequences for entire societies. Reconciliation requires that we come to see and love each other as equals. Jacob helps us to see ourselves and others clearly by pointing us again and again to God's inexhaustible love.

A third significant theme is the atonement. Jacob invites us to reflect on Christ's suffering on behalf of all humanity and demonstrates how the atonement evidences the value of every human being. The atonement can repair problems caused through inequality and lack of connection because it restores both individuals and societies who have been torn apart by sin and suffering to wholeness and reconciliation. At the same time, Jacob makes plain that individual agency allows us to choose whether to accept the atonement, as well as salvation. This means that each of us has a crucial role to play in bringing the atonement to consummation.

The book will start in chapter 1 with an introduction to Jacob and a few of his main concerns—equality, the dissolution of hierarchies, and his empathy for all people. We will then move in chapter 2 to a discussion on suffering with Christ and how Jacob has consecrated his own suffering to benefit others. Chapter 3 will explore Jacob's depiction of our spiritual lives as inherently social in nature and what that means for us as followers of Christ. Chapter 4 will discuss Jacob's temple sermon, in which he chastises the Nephite men for their poor treatment of children and women and decries the sinful hierarchies the Nephites have built around wealth, skin color, and gender. Chapter 5 focuses on the ways in which the allegory of the olive tree illuminates the atonement and how the atonement works to mend and redeem all aspects of human life. The final chapter discusses Jacob's hope for the future and why followers of Christ need hope.

1

Who Is Jacob?

As we seek to understand Jacob and his ministry, it is important to remember that all we know about Jacob is what comes from the text. We can read closely for clues, yet certain knowledge about his biographical, emotional, psychological, and personal spiritual realities remain interior matters that ultimately elude us. Although it would be impossible to offer a full reconstruction of Jacob, I offer inferences and educated guesses based on my own careful analysis. The close reading of the book of Jacob that I offer here emphasizes this book of scripture's continued relevance in contemporary contexts. I try to use Jacob's own rhetorical strategies, which make the familiar strange and give us the opportunity to see the book of Jacob's truths anew.

Jacob is the younger brother of Nephi, whom Nephi consecrates as a priest and teacher over their people and to whom Nephi entrusts the plates prior to his death. While Sariah and Lehi give none of their four elder sons names that bear clear resonance with the Old Testament, the two younger sons who are born after the family flees Jerusalem, Jacob and Joseph, share names with prominent figures from the book of Genesis. The names evoke themes of covenant, gathering, and reconciliation. In the Old Testament, it is Jacob whose sons become the twelve tribes of Israel that will be scattered and gathered. It is Jacob who makes peace with a brother from whom he had been separated and whom he had come to fear as an enemy. It is Jacob who suffers the loss of his beloved son, Joseph, due to family schism. It is Jacob who lives to see his estranged family reconciled at the end of his life. And it is the very son he had once lost, his most beloved son, Joseph, who offers his entire family, without exception, a type of salvation that is both physical and spiritual: he saves his family from famine and the threat of death by sharing his abundant resources and extends the forgiveness that heals deep wounds and makes reconciliation possible with the family that had once disposed of him and left him for dead. In the Book of Mormon, Jacob, the son of Sariah and Lehi, assumes a concern with the ongoing process of gathering Israel and the task of reconciliation in ways that reflect his ancestor and namesake.

As the firstborn son to Sariah and Lehi in the wilderness after they left Jerusalem, Jacob lives a life characterized by struggle and ambiguity. Lehi specifically identifies Jacob as his "firstborn in the days of [his] tribulation in the wilderness" (2 Ne. 1:2). Jacob begins his life in the midst of his parents' suffering and uncertainty, their wilderness. On Jacob's account, he was born not only in a wilderness but in a "wild wilderness."[1] Thus, Jacob is born into the unfamiliar and alien, which remains perpetually unpredictable, untamed, and unmastered. In the Old Testament, the wilderness (*midbar*) denotes a region whose scarcity of water makes it unfit for settlement, a place that can be inhabited only temporarily. Figuratively, the trope of the *midbar* refers to a desolate area that remains in a "primeval state of chaos," evoking "fear and revulsion."[2] From the first mention of him to his own closing words, Jacob's life seems overshadowed by a palpable sense of vulnerability, as well as adversity and melancholy. Yet the transitory space Jacob inhabits can also prove transformative.

Jacob's vulnerability

Among the various Nephite leaders of the Book of Mormon, Jacob comes across as an unusually vulnerable figure. Jacob's many references to his own anxiety account for half of all the references to anxiety found in the Book of Mormon.[3] Going so far as to express anxiety about his anxiety, Jacob understands that his discomfort results from his profound love and concern for his people. He worries that his fear over them will outweigh his love for them. From the very first instance that his speaking is recorded in the Book of Mormon, he expresses trepidation concerning the Nephites' spiritual standing. "I am desirous for the welfare of your souls. Yea, mine anxiety is great for you; and ye yourselves know that it ever has been" (2 Ne. 6:3). Although his distress most often stems from his concerns about his own people, he continually chooses to remain in relation to them. Because he views his people's eternal welfare and righteousness as inextricably intertwined with their temporal welfare and the creation of a just society, he catalyzes his anxiety into compassion for the oppressed.

Our very first introduction to Jacob in 1 Nephi 18 speaks to his tendency toward empathy. Nephi observes the sorrow experienced by many in Sariah and Lehi's family as a result of Laman and Lemuel's bad behavior. Having detailed the means by which Laman and Lemuel have grieved their aged parents, Nephi comments, "Jacob and Joseph also, being young, having need of much nourishment, were grieved because of the afflictions of their mother" (1 Ne. 18:19). Jacob knows firsthand that the unforeseen consequences of sin do not remain localized but surge outward in every direction. This gives the reader an early glimpse of Jacob's sensitivity to the systemic implications of sin:

unjust actions lead to suffering that ripples outward with innumerable aftershocks.

Furthermore, it is possible that Jacob's angst and his empathy for others are attributable to specific events. The text suggests the possibility that Jacob may have been physically assaulted or abused.[4] Lehi acknowledges that Jacob has suffered *affliction*, which could refer to the physical infliction of pain, due to his brothers' *rudeness*, which could refer to violence (see 2 Ne. 2:1).[5] Such experience might have enabled him to empathize with members of society who had suffered similarly. Jacob embodies the compassion that "suffers with" those on the underside of injustice and unrighteousness, such as the suffering women and children of Nephite society who, like him, suffer because of others' sins, rather than their own (2 Ne. 2:1 and Jacob 3:1). This compassion is evident in his teachings, when he calls his listeners and his readers to account, making plain that neighbor love and universal equality are at the heart of Christ's gospel and that these principles ought to inform all of our daily acts and interactions.

Jacob as protector

Jacob's awareness of his own vulnerability and that of others may explain why, when describing the love of the Nephites for his older brother Nephi, he highlights that Nephi had been "a great protector of them" (Jacob 1:10). Jacob had been assured by his father Lehi that he would "dwell safely with [his] brother, Nephi" (2 Ne. 2:3). The fact that Lehi promises that Jacob will dwell *safely,* rather than simply in peace or comfort, suggests that Jacob feels unsafe with his family, and this possibly includes feeling physically unsafe (2 Ne. 2:1, 3). Jacob's own deeply-felt need for protection, informed by his anxiety, turns him toward the protection of others, a theme that becomes central to his ministry.

One scholar points out that the word *protector* occurs only twice in the Latter-day Saint canon, and in both instances Jacob refers to Nephi, echoing Lehi's promise to Jacob that he would dwell safely with Nephi despite having suffered previously at the hands of his brothers. This promise of protection is so much a part of Jacob that even his name refers to it. Against the typical meaning "to supplant" associated with the name of Jacob in the Old Testament, Jacob's name could mean "may he protect" or "he has protected," with the male pronoun referring to God.[6] Yet this double meaning need not refer only to God; one could understand Jacob both to have been protected by Nephi (as well as by God) and to have the divine calling to act as a protector. To interpret his name this way illuminates Jacob's position in the book named for him. At the outset of the book, this vulnerable religious leader has just lost his older brother, Nephi, and with him the assurance of safety and protection. With his suddenly heightened sense of vulnerability, Jacob does not seek safety by secluding himself in a shroud of silence and invisibility. Instead, he proves to be as courageous as he is vulnerable by turning the attention of the Nephite men, who are the most dominant and oppressive in society, to the most subordinate and overlooked, including the Nephite women and children and the outcasts and outsiders of Nephite society.

Jacob advocates for those who have been rendered voiceless and have had their agency and well-being compromised in a society that unjustly constructs hierarchies on the basis of wealth, skin color, and gender. By giving voice to the voiceless, Jacob's book demands our response to the issues that they face, which remain pressing today. Like the biblical writer James (whose Hebrew name was Jacob, incidentally), Jacob reminds us that our religion cannot be reduced to the otherworldly; the quality of our spirituality is measured by the way we both regard and treat those who, like the incarnate Christ, are esteemed as naught within human societies (see James 1:27).

Jacob as teacher

Jacob states early in his preaching that his identity as teacher necessitates showing the Nephites the consequences of their sin (2 Ne. 9:48). In the words that he personally records, we see that the consequences of sin stretch far beyond the individual into every aspect of society. Jacob views sin as a social and societal phenomenon, rather than an individual one, a perspective he gained through his negative life experiences. Although Jacob is commissioned by Nephi to speak of the sacred and spiritual, his primary focus is on the way that Nephite society functions (or rather, dysfunctions) on the ground. Refusing to sever the mundane from the celestial, Jacob assesses Nephite spirituality according to tangible earthly categories, including the division of wealth, the relationship between religious outsiders and insiders, and the harmony of family life.

Jacob is the first religious authority in the Book of Mormon who does not function simultaneously as a political leader (Jacob 1:9). This allows him to focus solely on the spiritual well-being of those in his stewardship and to pursue the unification of disparate groups by emphasizing their shared spiritual standing. At the outset of his ministry, Jacob reminds us that he is teaching the words of Lehi (2 Ne. 6:3) and that he keeps the record of his teachings on the small plates in strict compliance with the instructions of Nephi (Jacob 1:1–3). However, while separation from others was integral to the prophetic projects of both Lehi and Nephi, Jacob's efforts are directed toward the collapse of hierarchies and the deconstruction of categories that justify separation. Lehi and Nephi's separative impulses included their own kin: Lehi was commanded to depart from Jerusalem and Nephi later separated from Laman and Lemuel, effectively creating two distinct and adversarial societies in the promised land (1 Ne. 2:2 and 2 Ne. 5:5). By the time Jacob begins his ministry, he counts seven different ethnic groups among the descendants of those who followed Nephi when he separated from his brothers (Jacob 1:13). Resolving not to get lost in these distinctions, Jacob focuses on what these groups share alike, referring to all of these peoples as Nephites and distinguishing them from the Lamanites based only on their political and religious divisions (verse 14). While ostensibly this is a move toward simplifying the arduous task of writing, in the larger framework of the book of Jacob it illustrates one of many instances in which Jacob seeks to break down barriers between people.

Jacob further eliminates social divisions by insisting that his proud and presumptuous coreligionists look to the least likely members of society for spiritual instruction. If the arrogant Nephite men are going to experience a mighty change of heart that leads to righteous behavior, it is going to require that they first empty themselves of their arrogance by looking not only to Jacob but also to those they view as the least authoritative. Even more expansively, Jacob allows those who might be labeled "apostate" to call the Nephites to repentance. By teaching in this way, Jacob encourages the Nephites to develop meekness, a "particular spiritual receptivity to learning both from the Holy Ghost and from people who may seem less capable, experienced, or educated, who may not hold important positions, or who otherwise may not appear to have much to contribute."[7] The Nephites must divest themselves of self-righteousness, renounce their claims of entitlement, and disabuse themselves of the illusion that they occupy a superior social standing. Perhaps in part because he never experienced the prosperity and comfort of his family's abode in Jerusalem, Jacob seems to have no sense of personal entitlement and no tolerance for it in others. His convictions that human beings are inherently relational and interdependent, share in a universal equality, and are commanded to love their neighbors, seem to keep him from excusing himself from his divine vocation as teacher and priest—no matter how much anxiety this vocation causes him. Moreover, his own sense of vulnerability and his empathic nature attune him to the needs of those who are more vulnerable than he is and drive him to advocate for them.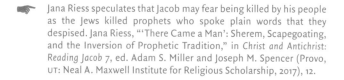

 Jana Riess speculates that Jacob may fear being killed by his people as the Jews killed prophets who spoke plain words that they despised. Jana Riess, "'There Came a Man': Sherem, Scapegoating, and the Inversion of Prophetic Tradition," in *Christ and Antichrist: Reading Jacob* 7, ed. Adam S. Miller and Joseph M. Spencer (Provo, UT: Neal A. Maxwell Institute for Religious Scholarship, 2017), 12.

2

Suffering with Christ

suffering, consecrated

Jacob's self-description as a consecrated priest and teacher seems straightforward enough (Jacob 1:18), yet his consecration is introduced much earlier in the Book of Mormon and in a more expansive sense. The first time that Lehi directly addresses Jacob is at the outset of 2 Nephi 2, in Lehi's great sermon on the fall and the atonement. Explicit about the firsthand knowledge Jacob has of real suffering through no fault of his own, Lehi promises his son that good will come of the suffering. He declares, "thou knowest the greatness of God; and he shall consecrate thine afflictions for thy gain." Lehi continues, "thy soul shall be blessed...and thy days shall be spent in the service of thy God" (2 Ne. 2:2–3). Lehi offers Jacob a redemptive framework through which to view his sufferings—those sufferings will not remain as wounds relegated to the past; instead, they will be "consecrated" in a way that will make them advantageous to himself and others. Jacob's written ministry is his effort to carry out and fulfill his father's blessing that his suffering will be consecrated.

To categorize something as "consecrated" is to convey that it is "separated from a common to a sacred use; devoted or dedicated to the service and worship of God."[1] This description further indicates that something is "dedicated to a sacred purpose; made sacred; hallowed, sanctified."[2] In discussing Jacob's suffering, Lehi implicitly endorses Jacob's perspectives long before the Nephites or readers of the Book of Mormon ever hear from Jacob himself. Jacob's sufferings are neither a hindrance to his perception of the gospel nor a matter of indifference. Rather, his sufferings play an important role in his ability to perceive and articulate eternal truths. This means that his sufferings are made gainful not only for Jacob himself, as Lehi overtly states, but also for all others who hear or read his words.[3] Lehi's significant, deliberate use of the word "consecrated" drives more directly at a distinctly Latter-day Saint understanding of consecration. Jacob models that a person's life can be expanded when viewed in a larger context. Jacob's life is not reduced to his own suffering, largely because that suffering is reframed as a means to understanding, instructing, and blessing others.

In a Latter-day Saint context, we can understand the consecration of Jacob's sufferings as a multi-step process of communal sharing. The first step is to give up one's sole claim to one's property—in Jacob's case, his "property" is his own experience. The second step is to give that property to any and all potential receivers within the community, and the third step is the reception of it by the recipients that constitute the community in which it is given. To this end, Jacob's audience helps to ensure that his suffering is not in vain by receiving the insights made possible through his life experience. In telling Jacob that God will consecrate his sufferings, Lehi speaks not only prophetically but also hopefully. As modern readers we can hear his words as a plea to us, individually and collectively, to benefit from Jacob by creating a faithful society through the means that Jacob identifies. Any suffering can be wasted, but it is clear that neither Jacob nor the God that he worships does so;

instead, both allow Jacob's unique life experience to fully inform his theology and ministry. It remains up to modern readers to make Jacob's consecrated suffering fully efficacious by receiving the gift through careful reading.

suffering the cross: Jacob and the cruciform self

Jacob's relationship to Christ is of primary importance to him. He is the first to use the titular appellation "Christ" within the Book of Mormon (2 Ne. 10:3), and he is named as a witness of Christ who has literally seen him, like Isaiah and Nephi did (2 Ne. 11:2–3), and who in his youth has beheld Christ's glory (2 Ne. 2:4). Jacob understands every aspect of Nephite religion to point its practitioners to Christ (Jacob 7:6–7), and he declares that the entirety of the prophetic tradition writes, prophesies, and speaks of Christ (verse 11). Jacob maintains that without Christ's atonement all of humanity would be lost, a truth he has attained through the Holy Ghost (verse 12). From the opening paragraphs of his own record, Jacob prepares his readers to understand his book by explaining that Nephi commanded him to write things that were sacred and revelatory and to "touch upon them as much as it were possible, for *Christ's sake*, and for the sake of our people" (Jacob 1:4, emphasis added). Jacob explains that he and others "knew of Christ and his kingdom, which should come" and worked to persuade their people to "come unto Christ, and partake of the goodness of God" (verses 6–7). Jacob avers that he and other Book of Mormon prophets "knew of Christ, and . . . had a hope of his glory many hundred years before his coming," as did all of the "holy prophets which were before us" (Jacob 4:4), and that declaring their testimony of Christ is the major purpose of their writing. It is fitting that one who enjoys an intimate relationship with Christ should seek to engender in his readers the desire and capacity for the same.

At the outset of his record, Jacob implores his readers to emulate Christ's submission to the suffering of the cross. Expressing the desires that underlie and drive his ministry among the Nephites, Jacob writes: "we would to God that we could persuade all men not to rebel against God,...but that all men would believe in Christ, and view his death, and suffer his cross and bear the shame of the world" (Jacob 1:8). Although Nephi makes descriptive reference to the cross of Christ and Moroni explains that the brother of Jared's writings were not to be made available until after Christ was "lifted up upon the cross" (1 Ne. 11:33 and Ether 4:1), Jacob is the only Book of Mormon figure besides Christ himself to explicitly call on followers of Christ to suffer Christ's cross and thereby to make suffering with Christ a required task of discipleship. Recall that in 2 Nephi 9:18 Jacob observes that the righteous followers of Christ can be identified as those "who have endured the crosses of the world" and that it is these individuals who will be received into the kingdom of God. Moving from observation to exhortation in Jacob 1, he calls all followers of Christ to enact their faith in this way. This recurs in the Book of Mormon only with Jesus Christ, who commands his followers to "take up your cross" (3 Ne. 12:30). Here, Christ elaborates on one specific meaning of assuming the cross: it is to deny oneself of extramarital lust, even if it occurs only at the level of thought, which amounts to a person having "committed adultery already in his heart" (verse 28). Likewise, Jacob presents a prescription to suffer Christ's cross at the outset of a sermon that is preoccupied with thoughts, including lascivious ones, and how thoughts affect the state of one's heart and one's actions. Everyone is expected to willingly suffer their cross by denying the temptation to regard others in a way that is faithless in thought, feeling, or action. Through self-restraint, followers meet Christ in the work of reconciliation, which is

21

crucial to a social mode of salvation and to the creation of salvific societies. Jacob, who sees that Christ's death on the cross is a necessity (2 Ne. 10:3), presents the atonement as something that Christians must participate in, rather than passively receive.

Beyond instructing his readers to engage in self-denial by symbolically taking up their own crosses, Jacob intriguingly emphasizes the necessity of *viewing* Christ's death (Jacob 1:8). The use of the verb *view* in the context of a person's orientation to the cross invites careful reflection. The word suggests an emotional interest in that which one beholds. In this verse, Jacob expresses a longing to influence everyone he can to explore the cross at length and perhaps even continually, not simply with curiosity but with a sense of personal investment. The operative definition of the word *view* during Joseph Smith's time was "to survey intellectually; to examine with the mental eye; to consider the subject in all its aspects."[4] Additionally, a sense from the Latin root is that of reaching or extending toward the object one views.[5] Jacob desires for everyone to contemplate thoroughly the multi-faceted death of Christ in a way that requires each person to reach or extend toward it.

Jacob effectively invites his readers to behold the death of Christ in order to "come to see this sight a second time" in pursuit of an understanding of what Christian atonement means and how that meaning pervades Christian existence. ☞ The repetition of our looking can allow us to see new things that will convert

☞ This phrase comes from Søren Kierkegaard's discussion of atonement. I interpret Jacob 1:8 as instructing us to continually look again in order to become converted to Christ. See Søren Kierkegaard, *Practice in Christianity*, trans. and ed. Howard V. Hong and Edna H. Hong (Princeton, NJ: Princeton University Press, 1991), 179. The phrase parallels Jacob's description of Christ as the Messiah who "will set himself again the second time to recover" his people, who wait for him (2 Ne. 6:14, 13). Together these divine and human actions suggest reciprocal and sustained investment in the relationship.

us further and draw us closer to Christ, both in devotion and likeness. This is to say that it is the viewing of Christ's death, which leads to greater understanding, empathy, and appreciation for his sacrifice, that in part engenders a willingness to suffer his cross. This activity might also lead to enhanced self-understanding. Because we cannot fully understand ourselves as human beings apart from our relation to God, knowledge of the divine and knowledge of the self are inseparable.[6] Although it would be counterproductive and harmful to look to the cross as our sole means of knowledge about God or ourselves, Christ's trust in and love for God above all else offers a model for one mode of human knowing.

In viewing the death of Christ, we understand that emptying oneself of selfish desires or one's nature, described in Christian theology as *kenosis* and epitomized by Christ's willingness to leave his heavenly glory and become incarnated as a lowly human and to submit to the most intense suffering in Gethsemane and on the cross, can bring us closer to Christ and closer as a Christian community. As a result of the closeness achieved through Christ's self-emptying and our own forms of self-emptying, which can include giving up our sense of entitlement to comfort and ease, as well as giving up our natural selfish inclinations in order to serve God and others, we can experience communion with divine and human others and gain new perspective (see Philip. 2:3–8, NRSV). The cross reminds us that even when abandoned by God and betrayed by human beings, Christ chooses to love faithfully and is motivated by this determination to endure these devastating experiences. Against personal will, Christ maintains right relationship with God (by asking for divine presence and submitting to divine will) and humanity (by extending love, mercy, and forgiveness; see Luke

23

22:42 and 23:34). In so doing, he models what it means to remain in right relation with both God and human beings, and therefore refrain from sin, even *in extremis.*

Throughout the book of Jacob there is a pattern of humility and deference to the other—the being that appears to be utterly unlike oneself—that finally culminates in relationships of interdependence and exchange as crucial to the life of faith. By responding to Jacob's exhortation to view Christ's death, a person can obtain a "hope in Christ" (Jacob 2:19) that she, through her reconciliation with Christ (4:11), can likewise live in right relation to God and all other human beings. For Jacob, this trusting way of relating to Christ and, in turn, to others relies on his view that Christ's atonement attends to the experience of all people in their various forms of embodiment and social standing. He carefully specifies that Christ "suffereth the pains of all men, yea, the pains of every living creature, both men, women, and children" (2 Ne. 9:21). Jacob's hortatory insistence that followers suffer Christ's cross, which entails experiencing the needs and vulnerabilities of all, must require as a corollary that true followers of Christ seek to alleviate the needs and excessive vulnerability of all. This aspect of suffering the cross is a primary theme of the book of Jacob.

A secondary aspect of Jacob's injunction to view Christ's death demands that we do not simply reduce it to the cross. Some Christian theologians assert that believers often move too quickly from the crucifixion to the resurrection, without adequately appreciating all that can be gleaned by reflecting upon the absence and uncertainty of what lies between Good Friday and Easter Sunday: the in-between symbolized in Holy Saturday. By viewing the duration of Christ's death, we witness and embrace loss that has not yet found resolution. Not unlike the wilderness in which Jacob was born, this middle space between crucifixion and resurrection is rife with contingency and unpredictability; however, this space also affords a love that remains even amid its weariness. Love's work is not limited to the sacrifice on the cross but is expanded to witnessing and remaining in a middle space. Theologian Shelly Rambo explains that in this context "survival is given shape through the curious imperative to remain and to love." To view Christ's death is to remain in Christ and to remain in love, even in the uncertainty of his absence and the indefiniteness of awaiting an unrevealed future. The divine absence and resultant ambiguity are not incidental but rather crucial to the Christian commandment to love. Rambo articulates that in the middle space, love is "birthed through a failure of comprehension." Within the middle space where meaning proves elusive, love becomes the "name for a series of relationships rebirthed in the aftermath of death." This love is "grounded in the process of speaking and listening."

Moreover, these two senses of what it means to view Christ's death—to be inspired to empty oneself of lesser desires in the struggle to remain in right relationship with God and other human beings, as well as to remain a loving witness in the middle space of Holy Saturday—both illustrate that divine love is "revealed at the point at which it is most threatened" so that love travels to the "place where there is no love."[7] Jacob's investment in setting Nephite social organization in order assures those on the underside of society that both God and followers of Christ will see and hear them and will respond appropriately. Divine love disrupts human injustice through the prophetic, cruciform witness that Jacob provides. What it means, then, to suffer Christ's cross is to follow his example by striving to remain in right relationship with God and human beings in all circumstances, maintaining a faithful and loving stance even in the face of uncertainty and despair. Saviors show the way through for others, and Christ shows all human beings how to stay in right relation even when it is most difficult to do so.

To engage the world faithfully necessitates remaining in dialogue with others. This type of exchange is not limited to words but includes being willing to see Christ in others and allowing others to act as revelations by modeling how to be faithful. As both a witness for and a type of Christ, Jacob enacts this suffering of Christ's cross as he chooses to remain in relation with, and avow the inestimable worth of, those who are rejected or ignored. For Jacob, Christian redemption occurs invariably in community and hinges on those who might seem least qualified to bring it about. Viewing oneself and all others through the death of Christ, one is humbled to recognize that all equally require what is brought about through Christ's suffering—all need the atonement as much as anyone else. When one views others and oneself through Christ's death, one sees the inestimable value that all human beings share in the eyes of God and Christ because Christ suffers to make possible an eternal relationship with each individual.

The inestimable value of each human being attested by the death of Christ includes the body and the eternal relationship between an individual and Christ that is formed through their shared embodied experiences. Also valuable is the knowledge attained through the body that cannot be gained in any other way. By emphasizing that the body is essential for attaining salvific knowledge and keeping it, Jacob helps us to better understand the importance of a literal embodied resurrection. He observes that it is only after those who have died have their bodies and spirits restored to one another that they will become "living souls, having a perfect knowledge like unto us in the flesh, save it be that our knowledge shall be perfect" (2 Ne. 9:13). For Jacob, there is a clear correlation between perfect knowledge and perfected bodies—the two go hand in hand.[8] It is only after we have gained both that we stand before God in judgment. With this observation, Jacob seems to presage latter-day revelation regarding human dependence on the body for obtaining and retaining knowledge: "Whatever principle of intelligence we attain unto in this life, it will rise with us in the resurrection" (D&C 130:18).

Although one might easily read 2 Nephi 9:13 to mean that in the postmortal sphere we simply retain the knowledge we gain in mortality, Jacob is at pains to communicate that intelligence is located within the body and that a resurrection is required to retain that intelligence postmortally. In other words, neither minds nor spirits are the sole location of knowledge; there is knowledge about how to be in the world that is received through the body and necessarily remains in the body. This teaching implies that some truths can never be extrapolated from our embodied experience into rational thought; rather, this knowledge is forever only available through the body. Strikingly, Jacob notes that in the judgment that follows bodily resurrection, the righteous—that is, those who used their bodies properly—will have a "perfect knowledge of their enjoyment" (verse 14). Jacob's insistence about the necessity of resurrection prior to judgment explains why it is the *resurrected* Christ who meets human beings for judgment. Christ too needs his body to remember the experiential knowledge gained through it in mortality; it is this knowledge engraven in his own flesh that allows him to view each human being's embodied spirit in all its specificity with accurate vision and mercy. Just as Christ suffers in and experiences the body in order to empathize with and judge us, he models for us how to be in the body—how to embody truth—in order to realize our divine potential as both individuals and communities.

3

Jacob's Social View of the Sacred

radical relationality and radical responsibility

Jacob holds a social view of reality that carries through his book. For Jacob, sin is societal and structural, so to be effective, redemption must apply to human life on these levels. All are implicated in sin and the suffering that it causes, even though not everyone equally shares culpability for either sinful acts or for social structures. Jacob's view of sin as social becomes pronounced when he warns the Nephite men to cleanse themselves of their own filthiness; otherwise, they will destroy their children and be held accountable for their children's sins. If you do not repent, he cautions the Nephite men, you will "bring your children unto destruction, and *their* sins be heaped upon *your* heads at the last day" (Jacob 3:10, emphasis added). At the same time, Jacob teaches that the Nephites, who have had correct teachings available to them for their entire lives, ought not to condemn the Lamanites, whose unbelief and hatred toward the Nephites are attributable to the "iniquity of their fathers" (verse 7). The Lamanites are not accountable to the same degree as the Nephites are because they do not enjoy the same degree of knowledge, through no fault of their own. This perspective will be re-echoed throughout the Book of Mormon, and

Jacob appears to be the first Book of Mormon author to espouse this view.[1]

From his earliest sermons, Jacob disclaims responsibility for the sins of others. By showing the Nephites the correct way to live, Jacob hopes to rid himself of the Nephites' iniquity and stand with brightness before God on the day of judgment (2 Ne. 9:44). Within the Book of Mormon, Jacob seems to be the originator of the idea that the blood of another can stain one's own garments unless one does all one can to make others accountable for their own sins. At the beginning of his temple sermon, Jacob explains why he has assembled the Nephite men: "my beloved brethren, I Jacob, according to my responsibility which I am under to God, to magnify mine office with soberness, and that I might rid *my* garments of *your* sins, I come up into the temple this day that I might declare unto you the word of God" (Jacob 2:2, emphasis added). Commending to them his own diligence in his stewardship, Jacob qualifies that, at present, he is "weighed down with much more desire and anxiety for the welfare of [their] souls" (verse 3). Prior to castigating the Nephite men for a number of abhorrent sins, Jacob makes plain that as their spiritual leader he is implicated in their sins, even though he is not culpable for them, and that their sins cause him suffering, even though their "abominable" thoughts and actions do not target him in particular.

Jacob recognizes that effective teaching is also performed communally. His personal ministry is consistently intermingled with others who serve as teachers. Jacob frequently employs first-person plural pronouns, even when it remains unclear to whom besides himself he is referring. This suggests that Jacob sees himself in such thoroughly communal terms that he feels no need to explicate that reality to his readers. Even as he invokes his own authority, he emphasizes that he shares his office with his brother, Joseph, who shares that authority (Jacob 1:18). He recounts, "*we* did magnify *our* office unto the Lord, taking upon *us* the responsibility, answering the sins of the people upon *our* own heads if *we* did not teach them" (verse 19, emphasis added). The work of reclaiming souls and creating a righteous society is not a solitary endeavor—it always involves a social component. Even his mission to call his people to righteous action is not something he accomplishes alone—Jacob depends upon God, his brother, and marginal figures to fulfill it. Jacob's dependence on others suggests an understanding of power, including divine power, that manifests as power-with, rather than power-over. Jacob understands that his relationships entail great responsibility, and he views his primary responsibility as setting all relationships right so that they may ultimately become redemptive.

equality: the fundamental ethos of the Book of Mormon

Closely connected to Jacob's social view of reality is his emphasis on equality, which is a fundamental ethos of the Book of Mormon. In the book of Jacob, the issue of equality is opened up to us with magnification and specificity. Calling out pride, greed, and violations of the law of chastity, Jacob's unrelenting critique of Nephite society also decries attitudes and practices that oppress based on differences in wealth, skin color, and gender, including double standards of sexual purity and agency. Jacob understands the root of all these sins as the failure to regard all human beings as equal before God, equally deserving of justice and love. Jacob insists that neighbor love is *required* for followers of Christ. That this type of love can be commanded implies that it is more a matter of action than of feeling.

The importance of distributing love equally is foregrounded in the Book of Mormon. The very first pages of the Book of Mormon declare God's universal love for humanity. In light of his initial vision, Lehi exclaims: "O Lord God Almighty!...thy power, and goodness, and mercy are over all the inhabitants of the earth; and, because thou art merciful, thou wilt not suffer those who come unto thee that they shall perish!" (1 Ne. 1:14). Elaborating on this viewpoint, Nephi asserts that God invites all people to "come unto him and partake of his goodness; and he denieth none that come unto him, black and white, bond and free, male and female; and he remembereth the heathen; and all are alike unto God, both Jew and Gentile" (2 Ne. 26:33). ☛ In affirming that God loves all human beings and wants all to dwell in the divine presence, Nephi articulates a truth about the divine nature that human beings are to emulate. "God hath given a commandment that all men should have charity, which charity is love. And except they should have charity, they were nothing" (verse 30). For Nephi, charity requires resisting the impulse to exalt oneself over another or make oneself great at another's expense (verse 29); further, one's charitable acts must be performed with righteous intentions and the right motivations (verse 31–32). Moreover, he warns that leaders of false churches deny the truth and teach false doctrine, encouraging their followers to perpetrate harms against their neighbors while assuring them that there will be no consequences for doing so (2 Ne. 28:8). Conversely, Nephi insists that after covenanting to follow Christ, one must have a "love of God and of all men" (2 Ne. 31:20). Demonstrating that he has

☛ Prior to this declaration, Nephi testifies of God's relentless love, especially through Isaiah. He closes his first book with the assurance that the Holy One of Israel will gather people from the "four quarters of the earth" and that "all nations, kindreds, tongues, and people shall dwell safely in the Holy One of Israel, if it so be that they will repent" (1 Ne. 22:25, 28).

appropriated Christlike love, Nephi testifies that he has charity for his own people, the Jews, and the Gentiles (2 Ne. 33:7–9). Nephi's final teachings reveal that becoming godly occurs by learning to love as God loves, that is, universally and equitably. While Lehi affirms the inexhaustibility of divine love, he never speaks about neighbor love as imperative for faithful living. And while Nephi does command neighbor love, it remains largely abstract in his teaching. By marked contrast, Jacob dedicates the breadth of his record to expounding how human beings ought to enact neighbor love on every level of relationship.

With the book of Jacob, then, we move away from the descriptive to the prescriptive. Jacob, like his father and older brother, is convinced of God's covenant love, but, unlike them, he dedicates much of his ministry to showing how the human side of that covenant is to be fulfilled. It is Jacob who presents followers with a full-fledged portrayal of what this looks like in human life. Drawing from both negative and positive examples, he demonstrates that society falls apart in the absence of charity and equality, which are lost when people are assigned disparate values based on identity characteristics. In Jacob's view, the most important manifestation of charity in human societies—the fruits by which love is to be known (see Matt. 12:33)—is social equality. In what must have seemed deeply surprising to the Nephite men, it is the Lamanites who offer a positive example of charity as equal regard of others. Despite their self-assurance of their own righteousness, the Nephites are reduced to a cautionary tale about how the absence of equality and charity precipitate familial and societal failure.

From Jacob's perspective, a recognition of the inherent equality of all human beings lies at the heart of neighbor love. Jacob queries, "those of you which have afflicted your neighbor, and persecuted him because ye were proud in your hearts, of the things which God hath given you, what say ye of it? Do ye not suppose that such things are abominable unto him who created all flesh? And the one being is as precious in his sight as the other" (Jacob 2:20). For Jacob, there is no criterion by which one human being can claim more worth than another. Pride in one's status or possessions is a form of sin and self-deception that God detests. As creatures who are all equally—and completely—dependent upon God for existence, all human beings bear the same value. Moreover, Jacob asserts that no one ought to think that riches or accolades exalt one over others since these incidentals are all attributable to God, not to oneself, and since none of these things signify anything about one's spiritual standing or personal worth. Jacob's predilection for the term "abominable" should not mitigate the force of its use here—God abhors whatever means human beings devise to excuse themselves from their obligations to every other individual. Disregard for the well-being of others, which results from misconstruing the source of a human being's value, gives rise to each of the heinous sins that pervade Nephite society; this is attested by Nephi, the son of Helaman, who much later names violations against one's neighbor as indicative of Nephite society's extensive wickedness (Hel. 7:21).

Following Jacob, the doctrine of neighbor love remains a strong tradition among the Nephite prophets. Benjamin makes plain that all are equally obligated to give the neighbor her due, and that what is owed to one's neighbor equates to what is due to oneself

(Mosiah 4:28). In Mosiah 13, Abinadi recites the ten commandments to the wicked priests of King Noah, including the commandment that one should not bear false witness against one's neighbor, and the commandment that one should not covet what belongs to one's neighbor (verses 23–24). In Mosiah 23, Alma₁ teaches his followers that "every man should love his neighbor as himself, that there should be no contention among them" (verse 15). ☞ In Mosiah 26, God tells Alma₁ the Elder that the people must forgive one another their trespasses and that the choice not to forgive one's neighbor when the neighbor says that she repents, is to bring oneself under condemnation (verse 31). In Mosiah 27, Mosiah₂ sends a proclamation throughout all the regions under his rule giving "strict command" to the churches that "there should be no persecutions among them, that there should be an equality among all men; That they should let no pride nor haughtiness disturb their peace; that every man should esteem his neighbor as himself, laboring with their own hands for their support" (verses 3–4). Observing these commands, among others, allowed the people to "abound in the grace of God" (verse 5). Finally, the resurrected Christ urges the Nephites to practice neighbor love and to go far beyond it: "it is written . . . that thou shalt love thy neighbor and hate thine enemy; But behold I say unto you, love your enemies, bless them that curse you, do good to them that hate you, and pray for them who despitefully use you and persecute you" (3 Ne. 12:43). Christ makes plain that staying in right relation to *all* others, even in the worst of circumstances, is a binding duty on his followers.

☞ Subscripts differentiate Alma the Elder from Alma the Younger for quick reference. Other series volumes employ subscripts to similarly distinguish other Book of Mormon figures who share the same name: Mosiah, Helaman, Nephi, and so forth.

Jacob's teaching of right relation is influenced by his desire to repair the breaches within Nephite society. Jacob is the most overtly committed to unity, equality, and neighbor love of any of the religious figures who influence the small plates. He does not justify or theologize separation but tries to return the people to the most fundamental truths about human beings and their relationship to God. Moreover, Jacob adapts his brother Nephi's teachings on equality, which include a specific reference to equality amid difference, as a means of reconciling the communities his older brother divided. By the time of Jacob's ministry, this division was reinforced by the Nephites' false belief about their superiority based on appearance. This desire to disarm the Nephites of their oppressive worldview, which keeps them at odds with God and others, may explain why Jacob devotes so much of his ministry to reminding them that no one is expendable by bringing them back to basics. He strives to remind them that two necessary components of a righteous and just society are love for the neighbor and recognition of human equality. For Jacob, both of these components are sustained by a state of mind.

love, a matter of the mind

The inextricable relationship between viewing all other human beings as equals and loving them as neighbors is reflected in the way that mind and heart are intimately intertwined. Jacob maintains that receiving salvation is conditional on the state of one's heart (Jacob 6:4), which for him is determined by one's state of mind. Jacob teaches that love is not an unruly, uncontrolled, or elusive feeling; instead, it is the result of decision. On Jacob's account, every sin in Nephite society results from the failure to see all human beings as equals. The prevention of sin, therefore, requires one to make a mental commitment, to view all others as equals and to give them their due. Loving one's neighbor as one-self begins with seeing one's neighbor as bearing the same essential value as oneself and as deserving of the same treatment. This viewpoint does not come about as a result of anything the neighbor does, says, or demon-strates about herself or her worthiness. Instead, it comes about as a choice to see the neighbor in a loving way in all circumstances—no matter how the neighbor may change or seem to change. Love is a just determinant for salvation precisely because it is a matter of agency.

Jacob makes love a matter of the mind repeatedly, and it is a theme that reverberates later in the Book of Mormon in more subtle ways. The way in which Jacob addresses this topic in the book of Jacob brings later allusions to the same concept into high relief. Jacob points to the spiritual state of the Nephite men as the source of his anxiety. He declares that although they had previously hearkened to his exhortations, he now finds the situation changed; they have begun to sin in their minds. Jacob asserts, "by the help of the all-powerful Creator of heaven and earth I can tell you concerning your thoughts, how that ye are beginning to labor in sin" (Jacob 2:5). Far from being benign or inchoate sins that one might consider negligible, sins of thought are, as Jacob confirms, grave: they appear "very abomina-ble unto me, yea, and abominable unto God" (verse 5). He continues that these thoughts are sufficiently ruin-ous to foster grief, a pointed word choice by Jacob, who believes that the thoughts of the Nephites are leading them toward spiritual death: "it grieveth my soul and causeth me to shrink with shame before the presence of my Maker, that I must testify unto you concerning the wickedness of your hearts" (verse 6). The sins that first appear as problematic thoughts eventually infil-trate the heart. Jacob's deep concern with unworthy thoughts stems from his understanding that such thoughts carry all the way down to result in actions and that their destructive effects proliferate. He unabashedly warns against the absolute damage that undue self-regard in both thoughts and feelings can bring about: "let not this pride of your hearts destroy your souls!" (verse 16).

Continuing to address the Nephite men in the temple, Jacob explains that because some have more material resources than others, the more affluent have come to "suppose that ye are better than they" (Jacob 2:13). This supposition hardens the heart, motivating words and actions that constitute persecution (verse 13). God condemns all of these as facets of the same sin; even the erroneous thought that one is better than her neighbor is worthy of divine condemnation (verse 14). Given immediately after this warning that pride can destroy the soul (verse 16), Jacob's singular admonition to prevent the pride that leads to soul destruction is as profound as it is pithy: "Think of your brethren like unto yourselves" (verse 17). Equal regard, which originates at the level of thought, flows into action: "be familiar with all and free with your substance, that they may be rich *like unto you*" (verse 17, emphasis added). By accepting the imperative to think of others as ourselves, choosing to see them as our equals, we will view them as equally deserving of the resources that we have. We will give of our substance to others, sharing all things in common (see 3 Ne. 26:19 and 4 Ne. 1:3), not because we view ourselves as magnanimous; instead, we will simply see all others as equally deserving of the same material goods that we possess. This is a logical extension of viewing others as our equals. All the laws hang on the two great commandments: to love God above all else with all that we are and to love our neighbors as ourselves (Matt. 22:37–40). Obedience to these foundational commandments and all the other commandments, which assist us in observing the foundational ones, are buttressed from the bottom up by the thought that all others are our equals who deserve the same treatment and material resources that we enjoy *and* that we are personally responsible to help provide.

There is another side, however, to the foundational commandment to love others as we love ourselves. We must also have a belief in our own value as a child of God and as an equal member of society who deserves support. When Jacob briefly directs his comments to the women and children of Nephite society, whom he addresses as the "pure in heart," he encourages them to "look unto God with firmness of mind, and pray unto him with exceeding faith" (Jacob 3:1). Continuing, Jacob sets before these righteous members of society a commandment to "feast upon his love; for ye may, if your minds are firm, forever" (verse 2). The provocative idea that feeling God's love is contingent on the firmness of the human mind implies that divine love is perpetually available to us, but it becomes fully palpable to us only when we establish certain internal conditions. In the context of Jacob's sermon, the righteous people who have been denigrated and objectified by the proud and self-righteous of their society may need to commit to loving themselves as they love their neighbors. Perhaps Jacob is saying that, while humility is crucial for salvation, a person must also have the self-love and self-respect to recognize her own dignity and worth. All of these mental commitments will be necessary because salvation requires one to "come with full purpose of heart, and cleave unto God as he cleaveth unto you" (Jacob 6:5). While God extends an unfailing, universal love and out of mercy "stretches forth his hands...all the day long" (verse 4), it will take proper self-love in addition to love for God to reciprocate the gesture. That is, in order to completely avoid hardening the heart, a person must remain open and loving toward God and others and also toward herself. She must value herself not only as needing but also as worthy of receiving God's redeeming love.

To know God's love is possible only through a change of mind—to alter the human tendency to establish hierarchies, allowing ourselves to undergo a divine leveling, evaluating ourselves and all others equally as creatures of God. This is no small task. Becoming like God calls for "the inner transformation of [one's] whole mind."[2] What Jacob clarifies is that this mental transformation involves abolishing hierarchies that produce misconceptions about the worth of souls, which is "great in the sight of God" (D&C 18:10), without any respect of persons. This unqualified, all-encompassing love is a divine trait that human beings must cultivate within themselves (see Rom. 2:11 and Alma 16:14). And while Jacob teaches that this process requires human decision, he also makes plain that human will is insufficient to secure the desired end.

Preventing wrong relation with God and human beings, whether it manifests as feeling entitled or undeserving, necessarily begins with a personal decision to establish a firm mind. It also requires divine assistance. Jacob attributes his own firmness of mind to God: the Spirit supplies the steadiness that allows him to carry out his divine calling. Just before his elaboration on the allegory of the olive tree, Jacob promises to unfold the mystery of atonement to his readers: "if I do not, by any means, get shaken from my firmness in the Spirit, and stumble because of my over anxiety for you" (Jacob 4:18). While other people's actions may destabilize us, by relying upon divine help we can regain and retain steadiness. Through divine help, we can overcome our mercurial human nature so that God can rely on us. This becomes evident in the comparison of the Lamanites who, approximately five hundred years after Jacob's preaching, are described again as superseding the Nephites in righteousness, this time precisely because they were steadfast. In describing Lamanite conversion, Helaman tells his readers that they had become "a righteous people, insomuch that their righteousness did exceed that of the Nephites, because of their firmness and their steadiness in the faith" (Hel. 6:1). It is their commitment to and reliance upon God, not their confidence in their own righteousness or in an established religious identity, that allows the Lamanites to remain firm.

In sum, what Jacob means by making our minds firm is cutting off sin at the level of thought. The moment we choose not to see *any* other person as neighbor, as inherently equal to ourselves, we are already existing in sin. The many evils in Nephite society for which Jacob excoriates his listeners, are, for all their variety, merely concrete, visible manifestations of a single, foundational problem: the thought that some human beings are of greater or lesser value than others. All of these sins are preventable through a decision to see all people as equal to oneself; universally loving action is a natural outgrowth of that view. This firmness of mind elicits the divine endowment of charity; this way of seeing ourselves and others creates in us a greater receptivity to feeling the divine love for everyone. In striving to become like God by choosing to regard all human beings as equally worthy of love and material goods, we come to increasingly experience the feeling of divine love.

In the following sections I will show that the principle of universal equality requires us truly to see all human beings as fundamentally neighbor. Even special relations such as spouses, children, and so on are neighbors first. This recognition allows us to see their fundamental worth and our interminable obligation to them. Partners and children are not commodities, possessions, or people less worthy of respect and esteem than others, and therefore the duty to love them never ends. Human equality, interdependence, and neighbor love are consistent themes running throughout Jacob's text. They inform not only the substance of his message but also the means by which he declares it. To better appreciate how these concepts inform the mode of Jacob's preaching, I will first analyze the crucial role of the Lamanites and Sherem in his ministry. I will then turn attention to the substance of his teaching in the temple sermon.

lamanites as revelation

Jacob deftly provides spiritual direction for those under his stewardship by offering it in ways that both humble them to learn from those they disregard and force them to recognize that redemption is a matter of communal exchange and dialogue. Jacob models this humility and interdependence by relying on those with less religious authority than himself to convince the Nephites to embrace the most faithful way of life. We see this throughout the book, but it is perhaps most pointed when he lifts up the Lamanites as examples to the Nephites and when he dialogues with Sherem in a way that results in mutual testimony. This mode of teaching reflects Christ's way of teaching and demonstrates Jacob's belief in equality before God, loving the neighbor as oneself, and the social nature of sin and redemption.

Recall that Jacob told his readers at the outset of his book that one of the things he would record on the small plates, would be "revelation which was great," which he would "touch upon...as much as it were possible, for Christ's sake, and for the sake of our people" (Jacob 1:4).

I suggest that one of these revelations that Jacob considers to be great is the example of the Lamanites' sexual fidelity. As he will model later in his encounter with Sherem, in making the Lamanites exemplary for the Nephites, Jacob uses divine inspiration to instruct his people to look to the archetypal other in order to learn how to live. Among the many reasons that the Nephites justify their feelings of superiority over the Lamanites, perhaps the most salient is that the Nephites believe themselves to be the faithful descendants of Lehi, in contrast to their estranged kin. In keeping with Jacob's pattern of taking every measure by which the Nephites aggrandize themselves and unraveling it, Jacob refutes the Nephites' false sense of self. Further, he reverses the false notion that the Nephites are the means of salvation for the Lamanites by showing the Nephites that they are unfaithful, and that the only way to become faithful is by emulating those whom they have labeled as the paradigmatic faithless apostates.

Blatantly upending the Nephites' self-created hierarchies, Jacob closes the part of the sermon focused on the evils that the Nephite men have introduced through aberrant marital and sexual practices, by drawing a comparison intended to cut them to the quick: "ye have done greater iniquities than the Lamanites, our brethren" (Jacob 2:35). Specifically, these iniquities include breaking the hearts of their wives and losing the confidence of their children (verse 35). As humiliating as this contrast must have been for the self-righteous Nephites, Jacob goes further by saying that looking to the Lamanites' example is the only way for the Nephites to get out of their sinful predicament. The Nephites remain in a self-justifying positive feedback loop in which the other serves merely to reflect their inflated self-image back to themselves. Jacob recognizes that the Nephites need the radical otherness of the Lamanites to see reality—and their place in it—accurately. The mode of revelation is not accidental: in order to live the life God intends, one must be willing to do whatever God instructs, even if that instruction comes from an unexpected or unwelcome other. The means are established by God no less than the ends, and, at least in some cases, the manner in which God reveals truth is calculated to help effect the change needed. If the Nephites are truly going to embody divine principles, they will need to first empty themselves of their inaccurate views of themselves and others.

Lifting up the Lamanites as the revelation of faithful community rather than reducing them to political, ethnic, or spiritual enemies, Jacob shows the Nephites that the other is to be received, rather than rejected. This includes receiving rather than resisting them as revelatory of how we ourselves ought to be. In the chapter following the sermon in which he unexpectedly makes the Lamanites commendable, Jacob writes that individuals should "seek not to counsel the Lord, but to take counsel from his hand" (Jacob 4:10). In the case of the Lamanites, the implication is that believers are to take counsel from God by putting aside their self-created hierarchies and being taught by those created in the divine image who may not have the expected social status but who enact the divine image most fully by choosing to love. Jacob's instruction shows that revelation teaches not only the *what* but also the *how* of godly living. That is to say that while each human being bears the image of God, this likeness ought not be taken for granted—reflecting godliness in one's daily life is the result of conscious choice and enactment. Godly living is a process of becoming, rather than a static form of being, and for this reason no one can afford to become complacent. This dynamic process of becoming requires that one be continually informed by other modes of living—by receiving and learning from the other—and appropriating what vivifies one's life of faith.

For the Nephites to accept the divine revelation being offered to them through the example of Lamanite society, they must recognize that, like all other human beings, they are less than the dust of the earth, divesting themselves of the status that they have arrogated to themselves. God never granted them that status, and it is one that God undoes through the very way in which God elects to reveal to them how to live rightly. Although Jacob denies that the Lamanites, and likewise Sherem, are *completely* godly (Jacob 7:23–24), he enables them to function as teachers of godliness, recognizing that because they bear the image of God, they can teach others something about goodness. As one Protestant theologian notes: "If we view ourselves as created beings, we see God everywhere; if not, then we see God nowhere."[3] To learn from the very other whom we would be inclined to dismiss requires us to remember our equality—to remember that we are all less than dust and are all dependent on Christ's atonement.

That Jacob intends the Lamanites to function as revelation is further intimated by his discussion of how the faithful are to relate to divine communications more generally. Following the sermon in which he lifts up the Lamanites as exemplary, Jacob implores his readers not to "despise" divine revelation, explaining that no one can know of God's ways except through this means (Jacob 4:8)—knowing how to love properly requires divine revelation. It is striking that Jacob observes a human tendency to respond with contempt or hate to love's revelations. In any case, the fact that Jacob immediately turns from lifting up the Lamanites as teachers of love to admonishing his readers not to despise revelation implies that he wants the Lamanites to be received as such. Jacob's desire for the Lamanites to be received as revelation is suggested in his use of the word *despise*, which re-echoes his vivid description of the sinful way that the Nephites regard the Lamanites. Just previously, Jacob rebuked the Nephites because they wrongfully "hate" and "revile" the Lamanites (Jacob 3:5, 9). Not only are the Nephites admonished to resist the urge to reject the form in which revelation comes but modern readers are asked to receive revelation from the most marginalized group in their sacred text, who are consistently represented as the paradigmatic apostates. To revile the other (i.e., the neighbor) can amount to despising the revelations of God and risks cutting off the possibility of rightly seeing both the neighbor and divine revelation.

The Lamanites do not have to get everything right that the Nephites get wrong to be a revelation. Note that Jacob enumerates a multitude of Nephite sins, but he does not describe the Lamanites as having practices and/or attitudes that are antithetical to each of them. The Lamanites do not have to outshine the Nephites in every aspect of their lives in order to prove revelatory for them. Jacob specifies that the Lamanites keep one commandment—monogamy and sexual fidelity within monogamy (Jacob 3:5)—and that they keep it in a particular way—with love (verse 7). Finding fault with the Lamanites will not free the Nephites from the standard that God directs them back toward through their example. The Lamanites do not have to be perfect—they do not even have to be orthodox or religious. They live aspects of covenant life in a way that excels the Nephites; the Nephites, therefore, are to be their students rather than their judges. Despite their other shortcomings, God, through Jacob, promises the Lamanites mercy (verse 6). Mercy is deserved because despite the Lamanites' resentments about their forefathers being forced to leave Jerusalem and losing political power to their younger brother, it is they who have allowed the new land of promise to fill the measure of its creation (see D&C 88:25) by magnifying the central commandment upon which this new society was founded: to practice right relationship within the family. Ironic as it may seem, the Lamanites do not live at odds with God's fundamental purpose for establishing Lehi's family in the land of promise. Even as the Nephites pride themselves on their righteousness and on living the good life, Jacob exposes that they do not keep the most basic commandment, upon which their flourishing actually depends.

With this example of the Lamanites, and with others, Jacob typifies Jesus Christ by giving voice to and lifting up the outcast as a divine teacher (see, for example, Luke 7:36–50 and Luke 18:9–14). Within the Book of Mormon, the resurrected Christ is the only other authority to make an outsider to Nephite society (and that outsider's teachings) normative. Recall that in 3 Nephi 23, Christ rebukes Nephi and the Nephite disciples for not recording the words of Samuel the Lamanite on the plates and commands that his words be included (3 Ne. 23:11, 13). Here, Jesus affirms that it was he who commanded Samuel to preach and further prompts the Nephite disciples to verify that Samuel's words had actually been fulfilled (verses 9–10). It is only Christ and Jacob who make the Lamanites, the quintessential other, an example for the Nephites' lives of faith. One scholar observes the following of the account of Christ's concern with the inclusion of Samuel's prophecy: "Laid bare here is a reluctance on the part of the Nephite prophets to include in their narrative something they themselves recognize as true prophecy, because, at least in part it seems, it came from a Lamanite." When Christ endorses the words of Samuel and insists that they be recorded, the "literal voice of God in the text singles out for distinction precisely the voice the Nephite narrative does *not*, at least not willingly, include—the prophetic voice of the Lamanite."[4] Although the Nephite tendency to exclude the Lamanite voice proves true overall in the Book of Mormon, Jacob's contribution to the Nephite record is an important exception which prepares the reader to receive Samuel the Lamanite as a religious authority. Far from being reluctant to give airtime to ethnic, cultural, or religious others, at times Jacob privileges their witness over his own. As we will see in Jacob's encounter with Sherem, allowing revelation to emerge from unexpected sources requires emptying oneself of personal will in order to fulfill divine will.

Jacob and Sherem: dual witnesses of Christ

Jacob not only commands his followers to look to their apostate brethren to learn how to live a godly life, he also practices what he preaches in his encounter with Sherem. Jacob's written witness culminates in a confrontation in which Sherem seeks to dissolve Jacob's testimony of Christ and discredit his teachings. Jacob's treatment of Sherem is unique in the Book of Mormon because, rather than silencing him, Jacob gives Sherem the opportunity to repent and to influence the Nephites for good by testifying of Christ and the atonement. It is Jacob's humility and love for his neighbor that makes it possible for Sherem to be an instrument of God. Rather than proving his spiritual authority by discounting Sherem, Jacob does so by helping Sherem to recollect and reaffirm the truth he already knows.

At the outset of their dialogue, Sherem states that he has made many previous attempts to converse with Jacob but up to this point has been frustrated in those attempts (Jacob 7:6). That Jacob had been inaccessible could be accounted for in a number of ways, but it seems most tenable that Jacob was somewhat reclusive, or at least introverted, a disposition that would make sense given the text's allusions to traumatic experiences in his early years, or it may be that his distress over his people's soul-damaging way of life drove him to seclude himself from Nephite society. Yet, his love for God and others, as well as his commitment to community, finally wins out over a seeming preference for isolation. Presumably, Jacob finally makes himself available to Sherem, not only to protect his people from false teachings or to reinforce his own ministry, but also to respond to Sherem's need. Implicit in their exchange is Jacob's underlying belief that Sherem is worth contending with—he is a soul worth saving. Jacob does not exalt himself above Sherem on the grounds of his priestly status or his commitment to Christ. He abases himself and finally comes face-to-face with Sherem in a way consonant with Paul's vision for Christian community. "Do nothing from selfish ambition or conceit, but in humility regard others as better than yourselves. Let each of you look not to your own interests, but to the interests of others" (Philip. 2:3–4, NRSV). The final result is a dual witness of Christ, made possible as Jacob and Sherem willingly remain in dialogue so that the divine will can work through both of them to accomplish its own pleasure rather than either of the outcomes that Jacob or Sherem anticipated.

Jacob insists that it is God who works in him throughout his encounter with Sherem. Recounting Sherem's affront, Jacob depicts divine intercession: "the Lord God poured in his Spirit into my soul, insomuch that I did confound him in all his words" (Jacob 7:8). Willing to treat Sherem as a spiritual equal, Jacob's self-emptying gesture invites God to fill him. This emptying of self, followed by an inpouring of divine power, will take place at least once more. Jacob further demonstrates humility in his response to Sherem's demand for a sign by the Holy Ghost, whom Jacob believes to be the source of his power: "What am I that I should tempt God to show unto thee a sign in the thing which thou knowest to be true?" (verse 14).[5] Rather than asserting his authority as a priest and teacher or calling Sherem's bluff by invoking a divine manifestation, Jacob simply acknowledges his place in relation to God by affirming his own nothingness. He further states his submission to God, clearly re-echoing Christ's prayer in Gethsemane: "thy will, O Lord, be done, and not mine" (verse 14).[5] Jacob is clear that it is only after he empties himself of pride, self-assertion, and his own will—which in this case was to resist Sherem's request for a sign (verses 13–14)—that "the power of the Lord came upon [Sherem]" (verse 18). By acknowledging his own nothingness, emptying himself of ego and self-willfulness, and suppressing the urge to make the focus of the interaction his own authority rather than Sherem's soul or God's truth, Jacob becomes an instrument of divine power. In so doing, he enables Sherem to become God's instrument as well.

In contrast, divine power confronts Sherem in a way that demands his humility rather than allowing him to experience this power in response to his humility. Jacob explains that "the power of the Lord came upon" Sherem and he was "nourished for the space of many days" (Jacob 7:15). After this time of nourishment, Sherem recognizes that he is going to die and asks that the people be gathered to hear him speak. His speech constitutes a self-emptying, both in content and form. Jacob tells his readers that Sherem "spake plainly unto [the Nephites] and denied the things which he had taught them, and confessed the Christ, and the power of the Holy Ghost, and the ministering of angels" (verse 17). Negating himself and his former position, Sherem tries to cancel out his deceptive and malicious way of being among the Nephite people. Emptying himself of the untruth around which he had constructed his identity, he is filled with the truth of Christ and the Spirit. Admitting that he has been deceived, Sherem expresses the utmost humility by anticipating eternal punishment (verse 18)—a drastic reversal considering he came onto the scene attempting to prove that the Nephite priest was perverting the right way of God (verse 7). At this point, Jacob's depiction of Sherem's speech and actions moves to figure self-emptying in an even more literal way: "when he had said these words he could say no more, and he gave up the ghost" (verse 20). Sherem not only empties himself of his arrogance and lies but also says all that he can possibly say to right his wrongs and confess Christ. At last, when there is nothing left to say, his spirit evacuates his body, expended in conviction.

Jacob's self-emptying facilitates Sherem's self-emptying, which further effects the Nephite people's own encounter with the divine. As the Nephites witness Sherem pouring out his testimony of Christ until his dying breath, "the power of God came down upon them, and they were overcome that they fell to the earth" (Jacob 7:21). The Nephites' experience of God is preceded by purging themselves of their preconceived notions about Sherem, so that the pattern is repeated: "when the multitude had witnessed that he spake these things as he was about to give up the ghost, they were astonished exceedingly" (verse 21). Only by being emptied of their limited—and limiting—conception of who Sherem was and what he would say could the Nephites be changed by his testimony. On Jacob's own account, it is not Jacob, but Sherem, a person positioned as his enemy, whose testimony accomplishes a reconversion of the people (verses 16–17, 23). Witnessing Sherem's confession, which resulted from Jacob rightly relating to God, himself, and his neighbors, sets the Nephites in a state of right relationship: "peace and the love of God was restored again among the people, and they searched the scriptures" (verse 23). Jacob avers that this conclusion was brought about through divine help, which he sought because he realized that he could not manage the situation alone (verse 22). Sherem's revelatory capacity is realized only as Jacob aligns his desire with divine desire. Jacob's unfailing love for God and neighbor allows divine power, not his own, to bring the story to consummation. Jacob's humility before Sherem and the Nephites eventually elicits their humility, which allows reconversion.

Allowing divine power to do its work requires Jacob to remain with Sherem, as witness oriented in love toward both God and neighbor. Jacob's sense of responsibility to God and others includes a responsibility to Sherem, to remind him of the truth that Sherem already knows (Jacob 7:14, 18). Through this relationship, Jacob teaches us that love disallows the beloved to dwell in self-deception and refuses to collude in it. Self-deception, like all other sins, is inherently social, implicating and harming others as it seeks self-gratification. Jacob's Christlike love cannot tolerate delusion, and this love fortifies him against Sherem's attempts to make Jacob question his own reality (see also Alma 30:16). Jacob resists Sherem's attempts to undercut his testimony by remaining grounded in God; this groundedness further allows Jacob to disabuse Sherem of the lie in which he lives.[6] By witnessing to—and ultimately with—Sherem, Jacob's sense of loving responsibility to others entails calling them to account for the truth that they know. Jacob and Sherem's interaction implies that it is impossible to redeem aspects of reality that one refuses to see and name. Jacob helps reconcile Sherem to reality by resisting Sherem's enticement to deny it (Jacob 7:10–12). Had Jacob been unwilling to see the true self and belief that underlie Sherem's façade, out of a shallow notion of charity as mere tolerance, Jacob could not have helped him to finally return to acknowledging that Christ exists and that salvation comes only through him. The testimony of one who has known the truth, has subsequently deceived himself and others, and has finally been reminded of that truth is potent for all who hear it. This hearing becomes possible only through a witnessing that evolves into interwoven testimonies. The dual testament of Christ that comes about through Jacob's prophetic exchange with his antagonist would have been precluded had he silenced Sherem's doubt and questioning out of fear.

The singularity of Jacob's willingness to give Sherem voice becomes more evident in comparison to the two other accounts of those who deny Christ among the Nephites, particularly Korihor. Although Korihor merits the moniker "anti-Christ" (Alma 30:6, 12), Jacob never labels Sherem in this restrictive way. Another contrast between the prophets' encounters with Sherem and Korihor is that Alma$_2$ strikes Korihor dumb so that he can no longer speak (verses 49–50). For this reason, when Korihor comes to himself and remembers the religious truths he had known prior to being diabolically deceived, Korihor can only write his testimony to the chief judge before whom he stands (verses 52–53); the text does not indicate that this testimony is made public in any way (verse 57). After praying for the curse to be removed from Korihor at Korihor's own request, Alma$_2$ pronounces that Korihor will remain dumb because he would deceive the people again were his speaking capacity to be restored (verses 54–56). Korihor is reduced to a cautionary tale; he is literally silenced as one oppositional to the community of believers until he is trampled to death, a fate that the text causally ties to his earlier choices (verses 58–60). Similarly, Nehor is taken by the Nephites to a hill where he is killed or, to be precise, where he suffers "an ignominious death" (Alma 1:15). Whereas Nehor is condemned to die (verse 14) and Korihor brings upon himself his own tragic fate, Sherem gives up the ghost (Jacob 7:20). Perhaps it is partly for this reason that by contrast to Sherem's positive influence upon the Nephites, Nehor's death proves insufficient to end priestcraft or the preaching of false doctrines. Alma$_2$'s suggestion seems to be that priestcraft is a failing of a society of people who crave false doctrine rather than a problem traceable solely to the false teachers themselves (Alma 1:16). Similarly, after the death of Korihor, righteousness is not restored as a consequence; in fact, Alma$_2$ reports that he is sickened because of the iniquity that he continues to encounter (Alma 31:1). Sherem's confession uniquely effects the restoration of peace and righteousness among the Nephites;[7] in addition, Jacob's faith is reaffirmed and Sherem confesses Christ. I suggest that this is in part because Jacob sees Sherem clearly by viewing him through the atoning death of Christ. Jacob recognizes Sherem as neighbor and one for whom Christ has died; he further recognizes that he and his antagonist are both equally dependent upon God and the atonement. Jacob's account holds forth the possibility that remaining in dialogue, even with a self-styled anti-Christ, can prove both revelatory and redemptive for everyone.

Moreover, one must see not only Jacob's humility but also God's will manifest in allowing a figure even more marginal than Jacob to bear final testimony of the truth of the Christian gospel. Jacob shows his love for Sherem in that he neither fears nor silences Sherem. He allows Sherem to become a teacher of Christian love by engaging with Sherem in a way that enables the divine to draw the testimony of Christ out of him. Significantly, Jacob's humility and sense of interdependence manifests in allowing Sherem to supersede Jacob in his own role as the teacher of the Nephites. Although the language of the text clearly alludes to Jacob's role as a savior figure, or a type of Christ, his self-emptying actions are consecrated to help Sherem redeem his own antagonistic actions by bearing testimony of Christ. Thus, the savior role is not restricted to Jacob alone but is consecrated and shared with the least likely figure in the text. In a moment of nearly unthinkable irony, the one who denies Christ as savior becomes a savior figure by witnessing Christ and catalyzing others' conversion, but he could not have done this without Jacob remaining as witness for and with him. Sherem's Christlike role is especially striking given that Sherem is not granted any special authority by the text, being identified only as a man who came among the Nephites (Jacob 7:1–2). We are never told that Sherem has any special training or status, yet Jacob, who has authority and status, relies on him to reconvert a people that he cannot convert on his own. Because Sherem's confession is so unexpected, the Nephites can hear a familiar gospel message in a new way, affording fresh possibility for their conversion.

Further instructive is that God elects to use not only Jacob but also Sherem to convert the Nephite people. While Jacob is humble in seeking divine help, he also is humbled by the way in which it manifests. That Jacob is willing not only to school Sherem but to be schooled by him is clear in the fact that he quotes Sherem's testimony verbatim in his book, rather than simply summarizing or omitting it altogether. Jacob does not edit the story to make himself the hero; instead, he organizes the text so as to make Sherem's testimony of Christ the final expression of Christian faith in his book, rather than privileging his own. That Jacob has the humility to let Sherem influence the Nephites for good demonstrates that the interdependence born of humility is essential to Christian redemption.

In lifting up the Lamanites as a vision of godly society and in allowing Sherem to function as a second witness of Christ along with himself, Jacob demonstrates that setting relationships right with God, self, and the neighbor often requires social reversals. As Jacob will make plain in his use of the allegory of the olive tree, the flourishing of the tame olive tree depends upon its acceptance of the wild branches. Receiving the paradigmatic other as a revelation for one's own righteous living requires a self-emptying that prioritizes the desire for divine truth over one's own will, modeled by Jacob's humility in engaging these teachers and engendered by the very act of the Nephites receiving them as such. Because Jacob does not exalt himself above others or excuse himself from all that the commandments require of him and his wayward people, he shows that it is when he becomes most fully emptied that the notion of community is most robustly fulfilled. This humble recognition of total dependence on God and interdependence with others in the work of redemption is something his ministry continually seeks to cultivate in others.

4

The Temple Sermon

Jacob's temple sermon, comprising Jacob 2–3, constitutes a passionate plea for justice and neighbor love and condemns the Nephites' faithless practices. In this sermon, Jacob's righteous indignation collides with the Nephite men's self-righteousness, which he seeks to dismantle by undoing their faulty logic, identifying their misperceptions, and decrying their mistreatment of women, children, and the Lamanites. Jacob pushes against their atomistic view of the self, which allows them to do harm without recognizing the consequences for themselves and others. He strives to convert the Nephite men to a social view of the sacred, in which human interconnectedness and equality, as well as humility, would guide their actions. Razing every hierarchical strategy of the Nephites, Jacob simultaneously builds a vision of what it means to be a human being in relation to God and others, and what a covenant community ought to look like. By devoting considerable attention in his small book to the way in which society is organized and how it functions, Jacob shows that our spiritual and religious lives are not separate from, but are actually realized in, our relationships to others, including on a societal scale. The very structure of the book of Jacob highlights the importance of this sermon's substance because Jacob both introduces and concludes his preaching with discussions of

his limiting task to write only things of sacred consequence on the small plates.

the relevance of writing for the temple sermon

Jacob underscores his sermon by enclosing the sermon
with two chapters on the importance of the written
record. Before delving into his oral discourse in chapters 2 and 3, it is profitable to analyze chapters 1 and 4
in order to understand how they frame Jacob's sermon.
In chapters 1 and 4 Jacob emphasizes the importance
of preserving the sermon in a written record by explaining that, due to the arduous process of writing on the
plates, he could preserve only his most sacred teachings. Included in his sermon are admonitions that
pride, greed, and social hierarchies that oppress people
based on appearance, gender, or financial means have
no place in a righteous society. These are teachings that
Jacob considered to be precious enough to preserve on
the plates, so we as his readers should understand that
these admonitions are of utmost importance if we are
to build righteous families and societies. Moreover, the
fact that Jacob recorded this sermon for future readers
suggests that he believed the sins that plagued Nephite
society would continue to plague us today.

Jacob begins his record by telling his readers in the
very first verse that Nephi gave him "a commandment
concerning the small plates, upon which these things
are engraven" (Jacob 1:1). Specifically, Jacob explains,
his older brother instructed him to "write upon these
plates a few of the things which I considered to be
most precious; that I should not touch, save it were
lightly, concerning the history of this people which are
called the people of Nephi" (verse 2). Clarifying that
everything in the book of Jacob bears deep spiritual
significance, Jacob elaborates: "if there were preaching which was sacred, or revelation which was great, or

prophesying, . . . I should engraven the heads of them upon these plates, and touch upon them as much as it were possible, for Christ's sake, and for the sake of our people" (verse 4). From assuring his readers that he has taken Nephi's injunction to heart, Jacob immediately turns to his preaching against the varied sinful practices extant in Nephite society. This sermon is the only clear instance of his preaching that he records in the book of Jacob; it is clear that Jacob considers its content sacred. Jacob introduces his recorded temple sermon with this reflection on his task as an author of the small plates, which is to record only the most precious spiritual teachings. Through this introduction, Jacob asks his readers to see that their way of relating to each other is the substance of their spiritual lives. Faithfulness, not unlike sin, is manifest in interpersonal dealings and the concrete structures of society.

Immediately following his record of the temple sermon in chapters 2–3, Jacob returns in chapter 4 to discussing the critical task of writing scripture, this time with an emphasis on the difficulty of engraving on plates and on their longevity. Jacob explains that he must exercise careful judgment about what to record. Emphasizing the significance of any words that make it onto the plates, he writes that it is only these words that will retain permanence: "we know that the things which we write upon plates *must remain*; But whatsoever things we write upon anything save it be upon plates must perish and vanish away; but we can *write a few words* upon plates, which will give our children, and also our beloved brethren, a small degree of knowledge concerning us" (verse 2, emphasis added). In considering which truths can insightfully inform the most pressing spiritual needs of his contemporaries and later readers, which he hopes will never be eroded from either the written record or human memory, Jacob gives priority to rebuking pride, greed, and sexual immorality, undoing social hierarchies, and challenging the inegalitarian family organization that formalizes the sexual objectification and commodification of women. Laboriously, he further records the faulty human thought patterns that give rise to these sins, which initiate the downfall of Nephite society and any society that fosters them.

Jacob 2 and 3 allude to the fact that God called Lehi to leave Jerusalem for the express purpose of not practicing plural marriage or intermingling with those who do (Jacob 2:23–27 and 3:5–6). Jacob attributes much of the sinfulness of the Nephite men to their own forgetfulness about this covenant. This forgetfulness is part of the reason why Jacob immediately turns from recapitulating his temple sermon to testifying of the importance of preserving divine revelation as written scripture so that it can never fade. However, Jacob points out that *having* written commandments is not the same as remembering or keeping them. Although the Nephites pride themselves on their special status as those faithful to the Lehitic covenant due in part to their possession of the sacred record, their self-righteousness relies on a convenient failure to remember all that the covenant requires.[1] In fact, the Lamanites who do not have access to the plates surpass the Nephites in fulfilling the covenant through love and marital morality (Jacob 3:6–7). This is because the Lamanites never stopped practicing the covenant, so the knowledge of the law remained in their bodies.

Jacob emphasizes the necessity of actively keeping the law in order to know its efficacy and remember what the law is. The Nephites demonstrate that intellectual knowledge that is not acted upon is lost: the Nephites have forgotten the covenant because they have not lived it, despite their proximity to the record.

The Lamanites, despite their distance from the sacred text, remember the covenant because they have lived it. At the time of his sermon, Jacob no longer considers the Nephites to *know* the commandment, stating, "ye know that these commandments were given to our father, Lehi; wherefore, ye have known them before" (Jacob 2:34). Although their knowledge *that* the commandment was given to Lehi is described in the present tense, their knowledge *of* the commandment is relegated to the past tense because they no longer live it. Jacob elucidates that while the Nephites have forgotten the law, the Lamanites have remembered it despite a lack of access to the written record and of a rehearsal of the law: the knowledge is in their bodies, not merely in their minds, and is therefore retained. Because they never cease to practice the law, it remains known to them. This is one reason, as discussed earlier, that Jacob points the Nephites to the Lamanites to show them how to live, yet he also records his sermon on his plates so that he will not be responsible if future generations of Nephites choose to forget.

Jacob's writings clarify that the very reason for Nephite society—and therefore the Book of Mormon — coming into existence has been undermined because the Nephites have not lived according to the Lehitic covenant. They have failed to record, remember, and live the strict commandments about family organization and sexual practices that God has given them, which would help ensure that everyone in their society live according to their God-given equality (Jacob 2:25–27). Jacob tells the Nephites that they have neglected the most fundamental principles: universal equality and respect for human agency. In Jacob's divinely inspired view, these principles entail monogamy, fidelity, and honoring women's sexual agency. He explains that a prohibition against polygamy was the reason Lehi and his family extricated themselves from Jerusalem. By extension, Jacob calls latter-day readers back to this most basic of tasks—creating a society with a family structure that is both loving and just.[2]

Jacob specifies that, in addition to preserving sacred laws and covenants, one reason the Nephite prophets engrave their words upon the plates is out of a hope that their "beloved brethren" and children "may learn with joy and not with sorrow, neither with contempt, concerning their first parents" (Jacob 4:3). Jacob wants his people, and his readers, to learn the truth about their first parents because it will help them create a more equal and just society that gives voice to marginalized people, especially women. Immediately after making plain that God called Lehi out of Jerusalem to create a new sexual ethic based on monogamy and equal respect for each partner's bodily integrity and sexual agency, Jacob informs his readers that not only he, but other Book of Mormon writers hope to vindicate Adam and Eve.

writing equality

Presumably, the prophetic figures of the Book of Mormon would have anticipated that much of the contempt of future generations would be pointed specifically at Eve, who has primarily been blamed for the fall. This belief has erroneously been used for millennia to scapegoat women for men's sexual sins and to delimit women's agency in subjugation to men both within and without religious traditions. Jacob's upbringing may have prompted particular attention to this misunderstanding of the mother of all living. Recall that in 2 Nephi 2, addressed primarily to Jacob, Lehi retells the story of Eve and Adam in the Garden of Eden in a way that resists misogynistic interpretations. He contextualizes the fall by enclosing it in a sermon about Christ's atonement and clarifies that it is Eve's actions that elicit the atonement and make agency and joy possible for all of humanity. For Lehi and Jacob, Eve serves as a type of the savior and is essential to the work of redemption. In Jacob 4, Jacob moves directly from his hope-infused reference to Eve and Adam to speaking about the atonement of Christ, followed by discussion of Abraham's near-sacrifice of Isaac as a type of Christ's atonement (verses 4–5). Like Lehi, Jacob vindicates Eve's actions as necessary, efficacious, and salvific in order to disallow justifications for subordinating women and commandeering their sexual agency that stem from less charitable readings of the Eden narrative. Jacob further articulates the necessity of his own efforts to write in a way that will prevent women from suffering injustice based on incorrect ideas about Eve.

Jacob's writings on the equality of women, and of all people, are intended to instruct not only the Nephite people but also his latter-day readers, creating the opportunity for us to apply his teachings as we form our families and societies. That Jacob and the other prophetic voices of the Book of Mormon would concern themselves so much with the social status of women ought not be surprising to anyone who appreciates the circumstances surrounding its provenance. During the incipient stages of the formation of The Church of Jesus Christ of Latter-day Saints, Joel's biblical prediction that people would prophesy in an outpouring of the Holy Spirit regardless of gender, age, or social class promised to be central to the process of restoration. Moroni recited this passage of scripture when he appeared to Joseph Smith to tell him about the plates that he would later translate to produce the Book of Mormon. Joel's prophecy reads as follows: "I will pour out my spirit upon all flesh; and your sons and your daughters shall prophesy, your old men shall dream dreams, your young men shall see visions. And also upon the servants and upon the handmaids in those days will I pour out my spirit" (Joel 2:27–29). Following Moroni's angelic visitation and through divine revelation, Joseph declared in 1823 that this promise was "not yet fulfilled, but was soon to be."[3] The translated text itself re-echoed the possibility of fulfilling this potential in its claim that women and children, no less than men, can speak for God (Alma 32:23). By giving voice to those members of his society who had been rendered voiceless, Jacob's contribution to the Book of Mormon text particularly paves the way for this possibility to be realized. Moreover, Jacob powerfully witnesses that God values women and children as much as men and that God is not silent about the mistreatment of any divine creation. This witness is amplified loudly as he advocates for the marginalized in his temple sermon.

preaching equality

Jacob makes explicit that his temple sermon came only after he "first obtained mine errand from the Lord" (Jacob 1:17). Part of what it is to love one's neighbors is to hold them accountable for what they know and not to condone their unloving and unjust actions. Jacob loves the Nephite men, so he holds them accountable for their unjust treatment of people whom they have seen as less than themselves. To counteract the effect of the sins of the Nephite men, Jacob consecrates his suffering for the gain of Nephite society by attending to those who are vulnerable and marginal among them. His attention and empathy lie with those who suffer for the sins and selfish behaviors of the most privileged. Jacob can empathize with this suffering because his own family was torn apart by pride and the desire for dominance. Presumably, Jacob's own trauma over separation impels him to subvert the problematic hierarchical values that hold these divisions in place. Toppling the false beliefs and self-perceptions that underpin the myriad social ills rampant among the Nephites, Jacob seeks to undo some of the damage done among Nephi's posterity by looking to the offspring of his more infamous brothers, Laman and Lemuel, whose practices edify and provide a necessary foundation for faithful life. Importantly, the entire sermon seems to rely on rhetorically invoking the Nephites' wrongheaded notions of hierarchy and then subverting their logic. Throughout the text, I believe, Jacob employs language that reflects the Nephite men's *misplaced* values, rather than Jacob's divinely inspired ones. If we do not read the text closely, we will miss that Jacob riffs on the errant perspectives of the Nephite men to reveal their absurdity rather than to reinforce them. If we misunderstand his rhetorical strategies, we risk justifying similarly problematic views and practices in our societies.

all flesh is of the dust

Identifying faulty self-conceptions as the cause of other sins, which manifest as various forms of misrelating to both self and others, Jacob introduces what will become the definitive understanding of the nature of human beings in light of their relationship to God. Since Jacob is the first to articulate it, his notion deserves close attention. In an effort to obliterate the Nephite problem of pride (Jacob 2:22), Jacob proclaims that "all flesh is of the dust; and for the selfsame end hath [God] created them, that they should keep his commandments and glorify him forever" (verse 21). Here, Jacob teaches that all human beings share the same status as creatures, owe God the same obedience, and bear the same obligations to love God with all their souls and their neighbors as themselves. Although Lehi describes the creation of Adam and Eve, it is Jacob who articulates the prescriptive implications of God's having created them out of dust, teaching both that human beings are all equally undeserving of the status and riches they arbitrarily confer on themselves and that human beings are all equally infinitely precious to their Creator.

Later prophets, including Benjamin, Amulek, and Helaman, develop these themes. Benjamin teaches his people that human beings "were created of dust" in order to make the point that no person can fully take credit for her accomplishments since she is reliant upon God for her very being (Mosiah 2:25). In his next breath, Benjamin argues for equality: "even I, whom ye call your king, am no better than ye yourselves are; for I am also of the dust" (verse 26). Benjamin seems to be saying that political hierarchies do not tell us anything about a person's essential nature or her status before the divine. Because all human beings are universally less than the dust and dependent upon God, no one may claim to be intrinsically worth more or worthy of more than anyone else. Amulek exhorts his listeners to humble themselves even to the dust and worship God, and to "live in thanksgiving daily" (Alma 34:38), suggesting that a recognition of one's own nothingness engenders gratitude for the unearned and unmerited gifts and mercies of God. Finally, the Book of Mormon teaches that human beings are *less than* the dust of the earth on the grounds that the dust complies with divine command, whereas human beings often use their agency to rebel against it (Hel. 12:7–8). The Book of Mormon's theology of human nature, building on Jacob, reminds us of our total dependence upon God and encourages humility, gratitude, a desire to be obedient, and a willingness to see life's gifts as graces rather than entitlements.

For Jacob, this understanding of the self also shows the grandeur of God and the precariousness of human existence. Speaking of God's relationship to human beings, Jacob expresses his wish for the Nephite men to experience some good old-fashioned divine humiliation: "O that he would show you that he can pierce you, and with one glance of his eye he can smite you to the dust!" (Jacob 2:15). God created you from dust and can instantaneously return you to that state at will, Jacob asserts. Further, he believes that all human beings would do well to remember this reality in moments of comparison that lead them to esteem themselves as better than others. We are all fundamentally created by God; our creaturely status is primary and precedes any other identity we might construct for ourselves on the basis of what we credit ourselves with accomplishing or making ourselves into.

Assertions about the relative nothingness of human beings set everyone on equal ground. They also encourage each individual to consider their own (universally shared) unworthiness before God, rather than comparing their relative worthiness to anyone else's. Jacob instructs the Nephite men he is calling to repentance to worry about their own sins rather than those of the Lamanites. He declares, "a commandment I give unto you, which is the word of God" not to "revile against [the Lamanites] because of their filthiness; but ye shall remember your own filthiness, and remember that their filthiness came because of their fathers" (Jacob 3:9). Beyond claiming that the Nephites have no less dirt on their hands than the Lamanites do, Jacob also offers a mitigating explanation for the Lamanites' unworthiness. In lessening the Lamanites' culpability by pointing out the fact that they have been taught false traditions, he seems to ask the Nephites, as well as modern-day readers, What's your excuse? Our essential nothingness reminds us that in relation to God, all human beings are infinitely far from God; that is, all human beings are fundamentally equal.

This humble view of the human person manifests itself in Jacob's self-perception as a mere instrument in the hands of God, upon whom he wholly relies. The first time Jacob is addressed in the Book of Mormon, Lehi proclaims, "I know that thou art redeemed, because of the righteousness of *thy Redeemer*" (2 Ne. 2:3, emphasis added). Neither Jacob's personhood nor his righteousness factor into the equation of his salvation—everything relies exclusively on the merits of Christ. This early insight into his relationship to Christ is reflected later in Jacob's sense of self in relation to the divine as he emphasizes that his words are not his own but those of God. "I must tell you the truth according to the plainness of *the word of God*. For behold, as *I inquired of the Lord*, thus came the word unto me, saying: Jacob, get thou up into the temple on the morrow, and declare the word *which I shall give thee* unto this people" (Jacob 2:11, emphasis added). Even in expounding the miraculous accomplishments of faithful individuals, which include receiving many revelations, having the spirit of prophecy, and obtaining a hope and unshaken faith such that the "very trees obey us, or the mountains, or the waves of the sea" (Jacob 4:6), Jacob is quick to explain that these abilities are actualized through God's power, not their own. "Nevertheless, the Lord God showeth us our weakness that we may know that it is by his grace, and his great condescensions unto the children of men, that we have power to do these things" (verse 7). Here, Jacob intimates that weakness is an essential aspect of the human person and that God makes it evident in order to show that divine power works through human impotence rather than removing it. To alter this weakness—or even an individual's recognition of it—would undermine the conditions for the possibility of the divine further working in and through an individual.[4]

In Jacob's case, human frailty is always apparent in his emotional constitution. Jacob knows that he is able to carry out his calling despite his overwrought disposition only because the divine supplies the grace necessary to hold him together amid the deep suffering and high emotionality he regularly experiences. He writes just before embarking on the extended allegory of the olive tree that he will unfold the mysteries of the atonement only as the Spirit offers him the strength to do so. "Behold, my beloved brethren, I will unfold this mystery unto you; if I do not, by any means, get shaken from my firmness in the Spirit, and stumble because of my over anxiety for you" (Jacob 4:18). Afflicted with so much anxiety that he experiences anxiety about his anxiety, Jacob returns continuously to the recognition that he, like all other human beings, is utterly dependent upon God for everything.

seek (only for your neighbor's) riches

In Jacob 2, Jacob pronounces divine condemnation of the Nephite arrogance that has arisen based on having more riches than another (verse 13). Declaring this arrogance "abominable," Jacob instructs his people to "think of your brethren like unto yourselves, and be familiar with all and free with your substance, that they may be rich like unto you" (verse 17). At the most fundamental level, Jacob is saying that all human beings are inherently equal, and all ought therefore to have equal material means. Insisting that the Nephites should seek the kingdom of God before seeking riches, he offers a single justification for amassing wealth: "after that ye have obtained a hope in Christ, ye shall obtain riches if ye seek them; and ye will seek them for the intent to do good, to clothe the naked and to feed the hungry and to liberate the captive and administer relief to the sick and the afflicted" (verse 19). Presumably, attaining hope in Christ involves recognizing one's total dependence upon God and Christ's atonement, remembering one's own relative nothingness, and as a result realizing that one shares in a universal human equality. Once the various aspects of this hope in Christ have set us straight about our own status vis-à-vis God and others, we may seek for riches—but to what end? The only reason to seek for riches is to ensure that our fundamental equality as human beings and creatures of God is reflected in our material lives.

What is labeled by Jacob as "abominable" is not specifically the state of having riches or even the action of seeking after them. What he emphasizes as problematic is imposing human standards of worth and ascribing to riches a sign of divine favor and superior standing. Mistakenly viewing riches as indicative of divine approbation amounts to a form of self-deception that justifies withholding material goods from those who have not. In order to stay in right relation with God, one must retain an understanding of one's own nothingness and equality with every other human being regardless of the wealth one has amassed; in order to stay in right relation with all human beings, one must consecrate one's material goods so that the inherent equality of humanity is reflected in everyone's material lives, regardless of who "earned" what.[5] One must empty oneself of a false sense of self-sufficiency to see that one has been provided for by God (verse 13), who has done so with the expectation that such provisions are to be shared indiscriminately and on the basis of need rather than merit. By divesting ourselves of illusions about merit, either with regard to ourselves or others, we free ourselves to pursue our God-given injunction to care for creation. Unhindered by false notions of entitlement, we can collaboratively create a society that works to meet everyone's needs through humble human effort.

re-evaluating darkness and light

Just as Jacob has shown that the Nephites' belief that their wealth signifies God's special favor toward them is faulty, he similarly denounces the meaning that the Nephites seem to have attributed to skin color. Although the language around skin color in the Book of Mormon might not present us with a perfect parallel to the contemporary world, Jacob's courageous and innovative way of getting the Nephites to question their facile hierarchy of light over dark can prove instructive for the present. In response to criticisms of the problematic language around skin color in the Book of Mormon, I consider how Jacob's discussion undoes the Nephites' faulty logic, thereby resisting attempts by future generations to justify racial hierarchies and paving the way for figures like the Lamanite prophet Samuel to have their authority recognized.

Although interpreting the discussion of skin color in the Book of Mormon in ways that bear implications for contemporary discussions of race will seem unsavory to some, I believe that we need to interrogate the text to fully appreciate how it can inform our lives.[6] In speaking about race, I do not mean a biologically determined reality but rather a social construct used to create disparate categories in order to justify relationships of domination and subordination. To say that race is a social construct is to acknowledge that conceptions of race have varied over time and context. For example, within the context of nineteenth-century America, Latter-day Saints were viewed as insufficiently white by racial supremacists, not because of their origins or appearance, but due to the fact that they practiced plural marriage, which was associated with cultures outside of

Europe and the Americas. Regrettably, Latter-day Saints sought to "prove" their whiteness through practices of racial exclusion in response to their experience of being racially categorized and marginalized.[7] These dynamics make evident the fluidity of conceptions of race and how shifting conceptions affect attitudes and behaviors. Acknowledging race as a fluid construct helps us understand Jacob's brief discussion of skin color as a vital aspect of his rebuke of the Nephite men. Naming racism as the most common of prejudices, one modern leader declares that *all* are called to repent for it. 🖙

Jacob's discussion can serve as a springboard for our repentance. Its potential to do so becomes more apparent viewed through the lens of Womanist theologian Barbara Holmes, who argues that outdated notions of race are reinforced by religious imagery that equates light with godliness, purity, and goodness and darkness with evil, impurity, and wickedness. Despite the fact that the Bible uses imagery of light and darkness with greater complexity—for example by describing the devil as appearing as an angel of light and darkness as the dwelling place of God, religious communities tend to be reductive in how they use this metaphorical binary.[8] For Holmes, damaging views of race are strengthened by this reductive use of metaphorical language, even when race is recognized as a social construct. Her insights show that our need to change attitudes about racial difference demands reflection on and expansion of our most fundamental religious imagery.

🖙 During the worldwide celebration of Official Declaration 2, President Dallin H. Oaks said the following: "Racism is probably the most familiar source of prejudice today, and we are all called to repent of that." Dallin H. Oaks, "President Oaks Remarks at Worldwide Priesthood Celebration," (address given at the "Be One" celebration in Salt Lake City, June 1, 2018), https://newsroom.churchofjesuschrist.org/article/president-oaks-remarks-worldwide-priesthood-celebration.

While some argue that discussions of skin color in the Book of Mormon belie long-standing American attitudes about the relative value of individuals based on skin color,[9] others maintain that these discussions of skin color are metaphorical.[10] Holmes invites us to consider that metaphorical uses of darkness and light might also entrench value systems that lead to harmful ways of relating to ourselves and others. Even metaphorical discussions might undercut the notion of universal human equality, a central doctrine of the Book of Mormon highly emphasized by Jacob. This possibility begs consideration of how darkness and light appear in Jacob's writings and elsewhere in the Book of Mormon.

The Book of Mormon demonstrates a nearly pervasive tendency to associate light with goodness and godliness and darkness with evil and wickedness. Beginning with Lehi, darkness is construed negatively and associated with Laman and Lemuel (1 Ne. 8:4, 7). Nephi, Ammon, Alma$_2$, Mormon, and Moroni all refer to darkness metaphorically to connote something undesirable, including divine absence. Deploying this dualism of darkness and light, Nephi asserts that God "giveth light unto the understanding" (2 Ne. 31:3). He also speaks of people whose works are in the dark (2 Ne. 27:27; 28:9) and those who choose works of darkness rather than light (2 Ne. 26:10). He makes plain that, by contrast, God works not in darkness (2 Ne. 26:23). Given this valuation of darkness and light, it is unsurprising that Nephi describes his vision of those who do not follow Christ even more pointedly: "they became a dark, and loathsome, and a filthy people, full of idleness and all manner of abominations" (1 Ne. 12:23). It seems to follow from Lehi's association of Laman and Lemuel with darkness and Nephi's vision of a people who became dark, that Nephi later describes the consequence of the Lamanites hardening their hearts thus, "they had become like unto a flint; wherefore, as they were white, and exceedingly fair and delightsome, that they might not be enticing unto my people the Lord God did cause a skin of blackness to come upon them" (2 Ne. 5:21). Regardless of how literal or metaphorical this discussion of skin tone is, the use of this terminology grows out of a basic binary that determines how readers see the relative goodness of darkness and light. This value system, which is imposed on scripture as well as informed by it, brings harmful repercussions to our view of race. Jacob makes efforts to resist this harm.

Although both prophetic figures preceding Jacob in the Book of Mormon, Lehi and Nephi, employ this binary, Jacob seems not to appropriate this view but instead to re-evaluate darkness and light. Jacob never uses terms related to darkness and light to symbolize relative evil or righteousness—this is his innovation. The only place in the book of Jacob that terms like *white*, *light*, or *darkness* arise is Jacob 3:8–9. Just previously, in Jacob 3:5, Jacob makes reference to the cursing of the Lamanites' skin. Perhaps the fact that he does not even engage metaphor reductively allows him to see righteousness and darkness as not being mutually exclusive. In the absence of negative evaluations of darkness—even metaphorical ones—the chances for misapplications of such evaluations to discussions of skin color are reduced.

Jacob commands the Nephites to "revile no more against [the Lamanites] because of the darkness of their skins" (3:9). Pointing out that the Nephites are not superior to the Lamanites, Jacob clarifies that righteousness is manifest through right intentions and actions, not physical appearance. Addressing the Nephite men, he declares, "wo, wo, unto you that are not pure in heart, that are filthy this day before God; for except ye repent the land is cursed for your sakes; and the Lamanites, which are not filthy like unto you...shall scourge you even unto destruction" (verse 3). Affirming that the Lamanites are "more righteous" than the Nephites because they remember to observe a commandment given to Lehi (verses 5–6), which the Nephites have failed to keep, Jacob questions his Nephite audience, "how much better are you than they, in the sight of your Creator?" (verse 7). The answer to this rhetorical question is clearly, Not at all. Skin color cannot justify social hierarchy, privilege, animosity, or abuse because that would deny the fundamental equality at the heart of Jacob's prophetic message and the fact that righteousness has nothing to do with skin color. But in case the Nephites will not relent their self-prescribed privilege on these grounds, Jacob goes further to wrest from their slippery grasp the very categories on which their hierarchy depends.

Beyond arguing that no one's relative value *ought* to be determined by skin color, Jacob shows that ultimately it *cannot* be determined according to this categorization, due to the total instability of the categories themselves. Jacob has already made plain that skin color does not indicate one's status before God by asserting that the Lamanites are more righteous than the Nephites even as he notes their darker skin (verse 5). He continues to utilize his temple sermon to dismantle problematic social categories by holding forth the possibility that the Nephites, who want to believe that their lighter skin secures them special status, could be "exceeded" by the Lamanites even according to the Nephites' own false constructions. In language that ought to be as discomfiting to modern readers as it would have been to the original Nephite audience, though for very different reasons, Jacob states: "I fear that unless ye shall repent of your sins that their skins will be whiter than yours" (verse 8).[11] Although suggesting that righteousness is reflected in skin color is both egregious and offensive, it is critical to note that Jacob seems to be working within his people's problematic assumptions about the world and their place within it in order to explode these assumptions. That is, he takes language that will gain the attention of the prideful Nephites because it *seems* to support their belief in their own intrinsic superiority. By relying on the Nephites' own conceptual framework, he follows a pattern of conveying truth attested elsewhere in the scriptures (see 2 Ne. 31:3 and D&C 1:24). Yet, he uses their language not to reinforce their faulty notions but instead to destabilize them. Jacob already made clear that he does not share the Nephites' views; he does not believe that righteousness and skin color bear any sort of relation to one another. Now he goes further by stating that their relative differences in this regard are neither static nor predictable. By implying that this category of skin color around which the Nephites organize their social world is subject to change and therefore artificial, Jacob leaves the Nephites with no justification for their oppressive thoughts, feelings, and actions. Skin color cannot secure social rank, according to Jacob, in part because the category itself is unstable. Jacob introduces this lack of fixity into the text, which I interpret as a gesture intended to problematize false claims to dominance and privilege based on skin color.

Whatever the given characteristics or differences that exist among individuals or ethnic groups in any given society, none are grounds for judgment, feelings of superiority, or oppressive social structures. Jacob declares that righteousness is determined only by those things that lie within our control: the state of our hearts, our thoughts, and our actions—the ways in which we relate to others. The Lamanites live in right relation, while the Nephites wrongly rely on characteristics, which they erroneously consider to be innate and unchanging signs of spiritual superiority, to justify and cover over their sinful ways. For Jacob, the righteousness of the Lamanites inheres in *what they do*; part of what accounts for the wickedness of the Nephites lies in an unfounded arrogance about *who they (think they) are.* This arrogance, which leads them to denigrate their estranged kin, further leads them to dehumanize their own partners and children. The terrible consequences of the Nephites' misunderstanding underscore the importance of using religious imagery in a way that reflects the complexity of creation and affirms the inherent goodness of every aspect of it.

grosser crimes

After condemning the systemic problems that grow from the faulty self-conceptions and values of the Nephites, Jacob laments that he must turn to a more sobering topic, which he dubs the Nephites' "grosser crimes" (Jacob 2:23). He considers their aberrant family organization and sexual immorality even more "glaring, flagrant, and monstrous,"[12] even more unseemly and shameful,[13] than pride or greed. Emphatically declaring that the Nephite men's failure to understand the scriptures leads them to justify immorality, Jacob inveighs against their misdeeds, which involve sexual sin and, worse, objectify and instrumentalize other human beings. The Nephite men view women as commodities that exist only to be used by men, not as persons whose desires, needs, and boundaries deserve equal respect with theirs. Of utmost importance to Jacob is addressing the Nephites' unequal and abusive treatment of women, which is their most serious sin and has caused immense suffering and the decline of their society. Bolstering his rebuke as coming not from himself but from God, Jacob asserts that his "people begin to wax in iniquity; they understand not the scriptures, for they seek to excuse themselves in committing whoredoms, because of the things which were written concerning David, and Solomon" (verse 23). Jacob's use of the word *iniquity* is deliberate given both its literal meaning of "sin" or "unrighteousness" and its etymology, which indicates a lack of equality.[14] Through Jacob, God without qualification or equivocation declares: "David and Solomon truly had many wives and concubines, which thing was abominable before me" (verse 24). Divine utterance does not stop there; it goes further to explain that the sum of God's intention in calling Lehi out of Jerusalem was to keep his family and posterity from such an abhorrent practice: "I have led this people forth out of the land of Jerusalem, by the power of mine arm, that I might raise up unto me a *righteous* branch from the fruit of the loins of Joseph" (verse 25, emphasis added). That is, the very reason God led Lehi and his family to a new land of promise was to separate them from the wickedness transpiring among the Jews in Jerusalem at the time of Jeremiah. What would demarcate this branch as righteous from those at Jerusalem, according to Jacob, is sexual fidelity within monogamous marriage.

Articulating zero tolerance for men multiplying their sexual relations beyond a sole partner to whom they are legally and lawfully married, God unabashedly forewarns that "I the Lord God will not suffer that this people shall do like unto them of old" (verse 26). In order to receive the blessings associated with the new land of promise, Lehi and his posterity must forsake and renounce the marital and sexual practices of their former home. God definitively states, "this people shall keep my commandments...or cursed be the land for their sakes" (verse 29). This clear divine pronouncement forces us to consider the possibility that the cyclical pattern of Nephite prosperity and suffering fluctuates on the basis of how women are regarded and treated within Nephite society; while these are a function of pride, it is crucial to understand that God loathes pride not only for its own sake but particularly for how it manifests as domination over others, in this case at women's expense.

Although God—through Jacob—is unequivocal that sexual and marital relationships between women and men are to be one-to-one, there is a single divine caveat. God may command people to practice plural marriage for the express purpose of raising up seed to God (verse 30). In the absence of explicit divine command, however, "they shall hearken" unto the commandment to make marriage exclusively a partnership of one wife and one husband (verse 30). To be clear, there is only one tersely stated divine exception given to an otherwise unbending rule of monogamy. While many Latter-day Saints are familiar with this pithy verse that offers exception to God's prohibition against polygamy, many fail to recognize the fact that this exception is situated in the context of an extended jeremiad against plural marriage—or *any* practice involving plural sexual partners—in which Jacob castigates the Nephite men for their defiant noncompliance with divine law.

Although Jacob allows for a divine imperative to practice polygamy, he never offers a positive example of the practice as a case of divine command, citing only negative ones. His caveat comes amid otherwise outright condemnation, and he gives no indication that this caveat has ever been concretely realized. Along similar lines, every instance of polygamy in the Book of Mormon serves as a negative example, in which plural marriage is condemned. In one instance, the pre-Lehitic community in the book of Ether is led by Riplakish, who "did not do that which was right in the sight of the Lord, for he did have many wives and concubines" (Ether 10:5). His descendant and subsequent political leader, Morianton, engaged in illicit sexual relationships that distanced him from God and became a source of self-harm. Morianton "did do justice unto the people, but not unto himself because of his many whoredoms; wherefore he was cut off from the presence of the Lord" (verse 11). One polygamist serves as the prototype of an evil leader in the Book of Mormon; King Noah is described thus: "he did not keep the commandments of God, but he did walk after the *desires of his own heart*. And he had many wives and concubines. And he did *cause his people* to commit sin, and do that which was abominable in the sight of the Lord. Yea, and they did commit whoredoms and all manner of wickedness" (Mosiah 11:2, emphasis added). Further, Noah excessively taxed his people to support himself and "his wives and his concubines; and also his priests, and their wives and their concubines; thus he had changed the affairs of the kingdom" (verse 4). These passages help us to appreciate why Jacob, with his social view of sin and redemption, is concerned about how plural marriage is implemented. The practice of having multiple wives can multiply sin and harm an entire society, including the initiator of it, unless carried out in accordance with God's commands. Yet, for Jacob, this seems to remain a strictly hypothetical possibility: he never offers an example, even from the Old Testament, of someone practicing plural marriage correctly.

In his own sermon, Jacob makes clear the importance of monogamous relationships, in which each partner has their sexual agency respected, when he says that this is the one commandment the Lamanites keep, and for this reason alone the Lord will be merciful to them. He declares the Lamanites to be more righteous than the Nephites simply because "they have not forgotten the commandment of the Lord which was given unto our father, that they should have save it were one wife, and concubines they should have none, and there should not be whoredoms committed among them" (Jacob 3:5). While the Nephites have forgotten the teaching they once knew and so risk their own destruction (see Jacob 2:34 and 3:3), the Lamanites still understand this doctrine and continually live it (3:5). According to Jacob, obedience in this one area is enough to offset their other sins: "now *this* commandment they observe to keep; wherefore because of this observance in keeping *this* commandment, the Lord God *will not destroy* them but will be merciful unto them, and one day they shall become a blessed people" (verse 6, emphasis added). The contrast between the Nephites, who are threatened with destruction for practicing polygamy, and the Lamanites, who God promises not to destroy precisely because they keep the commandment to live monogamously, indicates that monogamy and sexual fidelity constitute the fundamental commandment on which the blessings of the promised land are predicated (see D&C 130:20–21). Failure to comply with this command, Jacob warns, will result in the Lamanites destroying the Nephites (Jacob 3:3), which they ultimately do.

For Jacob, this fidelity and respect is a visible fruit of love. He immediately explains why he wants the Nephites to look to the Lamanites: "Behold, their husbands love their wives and their wives love their husbands, and their husbands and their wives love their children" (verse 7). Their marital relationships are reciprocal, sustained by equal regard. Moreover, Jacob indicates that expressing Christian love in this single area of human life through monogamy, unfailing fidelity, and respect for the sexual agency of all others matters enough to merit God's mercy toward all of their other sins (see 1 Pet. 4:8). In this way, Jacob connects two central themes of the gospel, namely the primacy of individual agency and the sanctity of family life, by showing that we must love and respect one another's agency within the family, including in the sexual relationship between a wife and her husband.

desire and revelation

In his writings immediately following the record of the temple sermon, Jacob moves to a discussion of how human desire impacts revelation. Jacob suggests to his future readers that, at times, those seeking revelation may be led into untruth, not because God wants to mislead them but because they want to be misled. Personal desire is one way that we might resist divine truth. Jacob reveals the danger of allowing desire to blind us from God's truth—we can obscure its plainness and doing so leads us to our own downfall. Jacob wrestles with the tension between the prohibition against plural marriage and the possible exception to it by making the practice conditional upon *divine* will, not human will. In his shift from preaching to his contemporaries about God calling Lehi out of Jerusalem to establish a society untainted by the practice of plural marriage in chapters 2–3 to writing on plates addressed to later generations in chapter 4, Jacob avers that the Spirit "speaketh the truth and lieth not...wherefore, these things are manifested unto us plainly, for the salvation of our souls" (verse 13). Yet, Jacob immediately explains how truth's plainness could be compromised. He explains that the people from whom Lehi was called to separate, the people of Jerusalem, were prideful, "and they despised the words of plainness, and killed the prophets, and sought for things they could not understand. Wherefore, because of their blindness, which blindness came by looking beyond the mark, they must needs fall; for God hath taken away his plainness from them, and delivered unto them many things which they cannot understand, because they *desired* it. And because they *desired* it, God hath done it, that they may stumble" (verse 14, emphasis added). Allowing one's own desire to outstrip the divine will can compromise one's ability to discern the truth of God's will—better, it actively conflates human will with God's will in the discernment process.

In his discussion of the fact that God will allow human beings to deceive themselves when they desire it, which directly follows his claim that plural marriage could be justified if practiced as the result of divine command (Jacob 2:30), Jacob charitably acknowledges human weakness and warns against letting it influence revelation. Recall that Jacob's first mention of the Nephites' problematic practice of plural marriage emphasizes their desire. He describes those he has spiritual stewardship over thus: "the people of Nephi . . . began to grow hard in their hearts, and *indulge* themselves somewhat in wicked practices, such as like unto David of old *desiring* many wives and concubines, and also Solomon" (Jacob 1:15, emphasis added). The problem here seems to be more than the practice itself; it is that the practice is instituted in response to human inclination rather than divine impetus.

This dynamic of divine communication responding to unrighteous human desires, rather than being initiated by God's righteousness, is attested in multiple passages of scripture. For example, God declares that disobedience caused the children of Israel to lose sight of divine truth and be overcome by their enemies: "my people would not hearken to my voice. . . . So I gave them up unto their own hearts' lust: *and* they walked in their own counsels" (Psalm 81:10–12, KJV). Paul's warning about the consequences of living in opposition to God befits the Nephites' sexual and marital practices: "the wrath of God is revealed from heaven against all ungodliness and wickedness of those who by their wickedness suppress the truth. For what can be known about God is plain to them, because God has shown it to them. . . . So they are without excuse; for though they knew God, they did not honor him as God or give thanks to him, but they became futile in their thinking, and their senseless minds were darkened. Claiming to be wise, they became fools" (Rom. 1:18–22, NRSV). Finally, in a revelation given to Joseph Smith, God declares: "if ye ask anything that is not expedient for you, it shall turn unto your condemnation" (D&C 88:65). To be confident that one is worthy to receive true revelation, one must first empty oneself of one's will in deference to God.

The Book of Mormon is self-conscious in seeking to pre-empt selective readings of its own sacred text that work to satiate human desire rather than to fulfill divine intention. The take-home message from Jacob seems to be this: failure to take at face value the overarching theme of equality and justice in scripture in order to justify selfish whims is destructive not only to one's individual soul but also to an entire society. Jacob indicates that his people did not succeed in maintaining a society based on a sexual ethic conceived around principles of equality. By calling out the Nephites' failure to live according to the basic principle of their land of promise, he also presents contemporary readers with an unfinished task. Thoughtful reflection on what went awry in Jacob's context can help us correct these mistakes and fulfill God's intention for covenant community.

the sexual agency of women
By naming the Nephite men's practice of taking plural wives and concubines as the worst of all their moral infractions, Jacob brings to the fore the crucial need for a sexual ethic that values female equality and agency

within covenant community. Concerned that women be recognized as full agents, both sexually and otherwise, Jacob states in one of his earliest sermons that women, just like men, have the ability to sin and are accountable for that sin (2 Ne. 10:16). Jacob views Christ's atonement as specifically redeeming the sins and healing the sufferings of women and children, not just those of men (2 Ne. 9:21). Jacob also intimates that suffering often involves being deprived of agency, since for him agency is a life-giving source of joy (2 Ne. 10:23).

My interpretation of Jacob's references to women's chastity in his invective against the Nephite men's sexual immorality is that he is referring to women's sexual agency. We must consider Jacob's pronouncement that God delights in women's chastity (Jacob 2:28) in its full context within the sermon in which Jacob re-emphasizes the Nephite men's culpability for the sexual sin in their society. Acknowledging that damaging marital relationships occur globally, God declares: "I, the Lord, have seen the sorrow, and heard the mourning of the daughters of my people in the land of Jerusalem, yea, and in all the lands of my people, because of the wickedness and abominations of their husbands" (verse 31). God clearly commands that both men and women practice the law of chastity, and God delights equally in the chastity of both. Yet here it is the men, not the women, that Jacob is rebuking for infractions against the law of chastity; while men can take away women's sexual agency, no one can take away another person's chastity because it is determined by consent. In Jacob's discussion of marital and sexual practices it must be the women's *agency,* not their chastity, that is at stake because that is what is being compromised by their male counterparts. God values both chastity and sexual agency, and if we do not read carefully, we miss this essential part of Jacob's message.

Jacob centers agency as the major issue when he, speaking for God, pronounces that the Nephite men "shall not lead away captive the daughters of my people" (Jacob 2:33). This pronouncement expresses divine concern about women being coerced by men. Beyond implying coercion, the language further implies the commodification and possibly even trafficking of women. Whether the captivity refers to a literal physical captivity or a more figurative spiritual captivity that results from being compelled to participate in relationships one does not freely choose for oneself, it is the sin of the men, rather than that of the women, that in this instance immobilizes women from being self-determining and carrying out their own wills. The reference to chastity cannot simplistically be intended in the way that modern readers might be inclined to take it—as virginity or as being sexually exclusive with one's spouse—because Jacob is castigating the Nephite *men*, rather than the women, for their infidelity while stating that something crucial is being lost by the women. He cannot call men to repentance for women's violations of the law of chastity; however, he can, and does, call men to repentance for violating women and forcing them into sexual relationships against women's desires. The Nephite men are robbing women of their God-given right to act for themselves, rather than to be merely acted upon (see 2 Ne. 2:16). So why does Jacob use the language of chastity here at all? Following a pattern, Jacob addresses the Nephite men according to their own value system (see Alma 18:24–28)—a rhetorical strategy he also used in his discussion of skin color. Their oppressive way of relating to others has led the Nephite men to so objectify and commodify women that at this point, an appeal to female sexual agency would probably fall on deaf ears. Yet, given that their oppressive ways include self-righteousness, the language of female sexual purity might get their attention. It is quite possible that by employing language that reflects the wayward Nephites' constricted values, Jacob hopes that his words will register, effecting the societal change that he is divinely commissioned to catalyze.

Furthermore, Jacob's language here is not meant to make women especially responsible for the chastity of all members of society any more than it is to equate a woman's value with her sexual purity. Instead, Jacob's language points back to the social nature of sin and the fact that the sins of one individual or group affect and implicate others in the sinful relations brought about through a single act. Perhaps Jacob's references to women's chastity are a way of saying that God does not want the Nephite women to be implicated in the social, structural forms of sin the Nephite men create when they compromise women's agency by commodifying them as plural wives and concubines. While not culpable for the sinful sexual practices enacted by the Nephite men, the Nephite women and children are profoundly affected by them—they are not just demoralized but to some extent incapacitated by the acts of others. This predicament could have been prevented, and can now be remedied, by an individual and communal choice to regard every person—including women and children, even one's own spouse and offspring—as neighbors. To do so is to view them as equals before God who are full agents deserving of equal regard. As human subjects (not objects), these neighbors have the right by their very nature to make their own choices concerning their bodies and sexuality, as well as otherwise.

Jacob's temple sermon addresses myriad issues in Nephite society, which have a common source: the failure to see all human beings as equally worthy of love, respect, care, material resources, and agency (including sexual agency). The theme of agency and the related notion of consent are so central to Jacob's theology that they characterize even a human being's relationship with God. His emphasis on this aspect of God's way of relating to us extends beyond the temple sermon and yet seems to respond to the need of each person to have her agency respected in a way that becomes clearest when considered in view of the discussion of women's agency in the temple sermon.

consensual salvation

For Jacob, this theme of agency, of consent, is so essential to faithful life that it characterizes even one's relationship with God. Amid his diverse depictions and declarations of God's love, Jacob is clear that this love is bound to us through covenant and remains within bounds by not overruling our individual agency. Salvation and eternal relationship with God are contingent upon our acceptance of God's invitation to relationship and our demonstrated willingness to conform to the divine life in order to make that relationship possible. Describing God's merciful and continual attempts to reconcile humanity to the divine, Jacob shows that these efforts are only realized when human desires are aligned with them. He specifies that "as many as will not harden their hearts shall be saved in the kingdom of God" (Jacob 6:4). In the Book of Mormon, human beings are always the agents of hearts hardening while God is always the agent of hearts being softened.[15] To maintain a soft heart when one could choose to harden it is a matter of human will. At least seven times within the span of just six verses, Jacob connects human will regarding the state of the heart with receiving salvation (verses 4–9).

Jacob is teaching that God redeems all those who are *willing* to be redeemed. On the heels of a sermon that is intended in part to remind the Nephite men that no godly society can exist without respect for the agency of all other human beings, Jacob reinforces its importance by clarifying that even God respects human agency because willing participation is a condition for right relationship. Rather than forcing redemption upon us by saving us in spite of ourselves, God defers to human agency. Although God's love is relentless and inexhaustible, it is not irresistible. God respects our right to choose, including our right to say no and to reject relationship. Individual consent, then, is essential to both social relations and salvation: God will neither save us nor impose divine love upon us without our consent. In fact, Jacob emphatically reassures his readers that this merciful and loving God who wills the redemption of all human beings categorically refuses to deny justice (Jacob 6:9).

That this respect for another's agency is an inextricable component of love cannot be emphasized enough. For anyone whose agency has been compromised in the name of "love" or "desire," for those who have had their bodies commandeered and exploited, for those who have been forced to "receive love" and "give love" against their will, there is solace in knowing that God does not demand or even ask that of us. Moreover, for those who have had the experience of having their agency compromised in any way by another, including in traumatic experiences, enacting agency positively to enter into relationship with God can be healing and empowering. Further, in making this point, Jacob provides a divine model for human relations—respect for the equal agency of others and the necessity of their volition is essential to those relationships. If God, to whom I owe my very existence and upon whom I am utterly dependent, does not and will not impose divine love upon me or force my eternal physical proximity to God, then it could never be justifiable for a fellow human being—who is no more than dust—to impose his or her will upon me. Whereas the Nephite men reduce the women in their society to objects of possession that can be easily commodified and co-opted, the God that those women and men worship refuses to render anyone as less than an agent. If God, who is not our equal, elects to relate to human beings according to a model of *power-with*, rather than *power-over*, how much more should we do so?

By looking at divine love in this way, we can learn not only about how to relate to all other human beings but also about how we ought to relate to God. Human beings ought also to respect God's agency or will in relation to them. The contrast between Jacob and Sherem as they relate to the divine proves revelatory here. While Jacob humbly invites divine will and presence (Jacob 7:14), Sherem demands and compels it (verse 13). While both individuals at least to some extent get what they desire, in the context of the encounter Jacob feels reassured of God's positive responsiveness toward him (verse 22), while Sherem finally expresses a fear of eternal damnation (verse 19). We might glean from this account that compulsion in relation to God fails to secure any sort of desirable relationship. From the divine vantage point it becomes clear that love can neither be extorted from another nor imposed upon another against her will: if it were it would cease to be love. Yet, true divine love remains; it is ever available, particularly through the atonement.

5

The Love of God and the Allegory of the Olive Tree

the all-encompassing embrace of atonement

As we might expect of one who designs his record in a highly Christ-centered fashion, Jacob devotes considerable space in a relatively short book to the atonement, incorporating this central event into his writing and preaching both implicitly and explicitly. Strikingly, Jacob says that because his people keep the law of Moses in order to point their souls to Christ, "it is sanctified unto us for righteousness, even as it was accounted unto Abraham in the wilderness to be obedient unto the commands of God in offering up his son Isaac, which is a similitude of God and his Only Begotten Son" (Jacob 4:5). Jacob is clearly interested in recognizing and figuring that which typifies Christ, especially in the context of atonement and reconciliation. He queries, "for why not speak of the atonement of Christ, and attain to a perfect knowledge of him, as to attain to the knowledge of a resurrection and the world to come?" (verse 12). Jacob offers an extensive view of the atonement, helping his readers to see that it has the potential to mend and redeem every aspect of human life.

Notably, Jacob emphasizes the promise of resurrection in his discussion of atonement. He sets before the Nephites an imperative: "be reconciled unto [God] through the atonement of Christ, his Only Begotten Son, and ye may obtain a resurrection" (Jacob 4:11). Jacob's formulation here gives the impression that resurrection follows and is conditional upon reconciliation to God through Christ. However, he previously taught that resurrection is universal, and, although it is made possible through the atonement of Jesus Christ, it is not conditional upon one's acceptance of it. In 2 Nephi 9 he states unequivocally that through the infinite atonement, "all men become incorruptible, and immortal, and they are living souls, having a perfect knowledge like unto us in the flesh" (verse 13). Since Jacob teaches in his early preaching that physical resurrection is universal and occurs independent of human choice, it would seem that here in his later writings he speaks of resurrection in a more figurative sense—for example, a spiritual resurrection of a person undone by sin or extreme adversity, or the resurrection that reunites a fragmented community. Through a desire and effort to reconcile oneself to God, changes effected through grace facilitate these other resurrections.

The reconciliation with God that enables multiple forms of resurrection depends on an individual's decision to orient and extend herself toward God and enter into a relationship that God has initiated and made always-already available. Jacob describes this reciprocal dynamic in a way that reveals both divine vulnerability and human empowerment: "repent, and come with full purpose of heart, and cleave unto God as he cleaveth unto you . . . his arm of mercy is extended towards you" (Jacob 6:5). God always-already extends open arms to all human individuals, who may choose whether or not to reciprocate divine embrace. This relationship is not inevitable but on the divine side remains perpetually available. Collapsing the space between God and a person, Jacob images the God relationship itself as one that brings the two face-to-face. Realizing the vast power differential between God and those whom God loves as divine creation, God's condescension makes the situation safe and empowering enough for human beings to enable authentic relationship. Although the divine decision to be in relation with human individuals is made prior to their decision, it does not override their ability and need to choose or reject it for themselves.

Beyond the reciprocal imagery, reflection on the use of the verb "to cleave" offers further insight into the God relationship. To cleave is to "stick; to adhere; to hold to," to "unite aptly," and to "unite or be united closely in interest or affection; to adhere with strong attachment."[1] God offers relationship to each person from a position of deep investment and emotional attachment. Jacob calls his readers to mirror this relationship by holding to God with a similar affection and interest in God's being. Jacob articulates clearly that human beings can avail themselves of the opportunity to reciprocate God's embrace only on the condition that they "harden not [their] hearts" (Jacob 6:5). To enjoy this state of the heart requires a continual openness to other people as well as to God, with all the humility, deference, and respect that retaining this openness demands. For Jacob, the only alternative to keeping one's heart in this state of softness is death (verse 6). Life itself depends on continual openness to others, both human and divine.

This openness, receptivity, and self-extension are no small matter given the devastating realities of human sin and suffering. Jacob reveals to his readers his special insight to the fact that, far from a trite or superficial notion, the scope of the atonement must be vast, encompassing the breadth and depth of human suffering and sin. In addition to his own experiences of suffering and his attunement to the suffering of others,

Jacob discloses an appreciation for the fact that the atonement of which he testifies must cover not only individual sin and suffering, as well as structural sin and experiences of oppression in the social realm, but also mass trauma, including traumas that take place as a result of intentional human action, such as genocide. Jacob relates that as a result of both "faith and great anxiety, it truly had been made manifest unto us concerning our people, what things should happen unto them" (Jacob 1:5). The destiny of his people, of course, would be annihilation by their ethnic and religious enemies. Jacob's overwrought, melancholic disposition, his own embodied experiences of suffering, and his deep empathy and concern for his people allow him to anticipate their fate—not only a life of unnecessary suffering caused by their own practices of injustice but further widespread trauma and ultimately, genocide. These anxious anticipations, however, also prepare him to understand Christ and his atonement in ways he might have missed without the vantage point of his tragic vision. As Jacob variously engages his listeners and readers to turn toward atonement, he is not merely seeking to show how it can cover some minor imperfection or impropriety. Much more expansively, he endeavors to uncover how the atonement can heal and redeem experiences of suffering and evil that remain nearly unfathomable to the finite minds of human beings. It is fitting that Jacob introduces the term "infinite atonement" (2 Ne. 9:7) to the Book of Mormon,[2] since he is the one who has seen with his own eyes not only Christ but also the depths that Christ's atoning work must plumb.[3]

allegorical atonement

Jacob senses deeply his responsibility to teach that the atonement is universally accessible, necessary, and efficacious and that it not only restores individuals and societies torn apart by trauma and sin to wholeness but also seals relationships with the divine and with others. He draws on Zenos's allegory of the olive tree to illustrate the atonement as expansively as possible. In presenting his allegorical discussion, Jacob informs his readers that he will explain the mysteries of atonement to them, bringing its obscure truths to light (Jacob 4:18). In his pathos-filled depiction of God's desire for the well-being and reconciliation of creation, Jacob shows that there is finally no place where divine love is not willing to go. In a sense, Jacob 5 resists a single, systematic reading as it seeks to make atonement intelligible in multiple contexts. The multivalence of Jacob 5 affords numerous possible readings; however, whatever else it may be able to convey or was intended to convey, it is ultimately about Christ and his work of atonement in reuniting the entire human family to himself, healing them from every possible form of alienation.[4]

Jacob 5 contains an extended allegory about an olive vineyard, much of which has become so corrupt and unfruitful that the master of the vineyard, who represents God, out of love, seeks to salvage and restore it to its natural fecundity. This allegory is most often understood in terms of the scattering and gathering of Israel as an integral part of divine covenant. It can also be read in more expansive terms, with the restored vineyard representing the integration, reconciliation, and wholeness that is possible only in and through the atonement of Jesus Christ for both individuals and societies who have been fragmented and disintegrated through traumatic experience or sin. This reading amplifies the breadth and profundity of God's love for humanity. Just as Jacob has shown us that all suffering and sin are inherently social, so too is the work of redemption. In Jacob 5 we read an elaboration of how it is that communities are healed and reconciled, and we avail ourselves of a greater appreciation and understanding concerning the fact that the atonement operates on every level of existence, reconciling individuals to themselves, to God, and with their communities. One explanation that accounts for the complexity, variety, and multivalence of this allegory is that the atonement meets each individual in her unique need.[5] Through this allegory, Jacob allows every reader to locate herself and her personal story of redemption within the text.

Multiple themes introduced elsewhere in the book of Jacob surface in the context of this allegory. These themes include an emphasis on interdependence that extends even to God's dependence on human beings to bring to pass atonement (Jacob 5:71), the importance of unity (verses 68, 74), and the significance of equality (verses 66, 74). Within this context, these themes return us to a realization about the relative nothingness of human beings before God (verse 42). We are reminded of the perpetual tension between the realization of that nothingness with God's refusal to view any individual as expendable. The high value that God places on individuals elicits divine longsuffering (verse 51) and nearly innumerable attempts to reclaim each soul while still respecting human agency (verse 64). Jacob's depiction of the labors of the master of the vineyard shows that the process of atonement—being restored to wholeness—requires both the agency of the individual being reintegrated and the involvement of someone external to her. While respecting the bounds of human agency, God affirms the divine desire to bring what has been lost or taken away back to its original state (verses 67–68). God's unrelenting love actualizes itself so repeatedly and variously that God asks finally, "What could I have done more for my vineyard?" (verse 41, see also verses 47, 49). God perpetually tries one more time (verse 64) and ceaselessly innovates to secure the fidelity of God's children.

Within his depiction of deity in Jacob 5, Jacob points his readers to the inescapable reality that insularity, in which we close ourselves off from other individuals and communities who are unlike us, will not save us, but that humility, reliance upon divine wisdom, and interdependence with others, especially with those most unlike us, can. God's covenant with Israel will not be fulfilled if those within the covenant isolate themselves from others. The tame olive trees that represent Israel (Jacob 6:1) cannot flourish or even survive without the new life introduced by the wild branches. Far from being disposable, the wild olive trees alone are capable of saving the tame olive trees from being deemed "good for nothing" and cast out.

Using this allegory, Jacob depicts God as one who is entangled, related, and implicated in the world's becoming.[6] In this dynamic, God's power is manifest through God's intimate connectedness to creation. Furthermore, God is vulnerable to the world, the object of God's creation.[7] Through covenant, the divine binds itself to humanity in order to reduce the human vulnerability in the relationship; condescending and immersing itself in an unruly vineyard, the divine both invites and respects human responsiveness. Moreover, God further becomes vulnerable by displaying a dependence on others for the fulfillment of covenant, including individuals who must respond to God's salvific efforts and the servant and laborers who work together to carry out God's efforts. Furthermore, like the tame olive trees that represent the house of Israel, God too is dependent upon the wild branches to help bring his purposes for creation to fruition.

In Jacob's depiction, the personal suffering God faces by confronting the potential permanent loss and separation of human creatures impels relentless divine labor to bring them back into harmony with God and one another. God is driven by a certain loving anxiety for creatures to continually call them back into the faithful life that affords reconciliation and intimate proximity with the divine. This extended allegory, in which God, through the help of Christ and others, seeks to save a perishing vineyard attests the inexhaustibility of divine love. In it, God repeatedly voices grief over the potential loss of any part of divine creation: "it grieveth me that I should lose this tree" (Jacob 5:7). Iterations of this poignant sentiment are found in verses 11, 13, 32, 46, 47, 51, and 66. Clearly, Jacob has a deep sense of God's emotional life and the influence that the experience of humanity's alienation from God has not only upon humanity but upon God. The moving language Jacob draws upon suggests that the process of atonement is designed to heal God's broken heart over separation from creation as much as it is designed to heal the broken hearts of human beings over separation from God and one another. Here we see that Jacob's constant concern over the righteousness of his people, which bears the potential to allow for the reuniting of his family, parallels his understanding of God's own emotionally laden yearning for ultimate reunion. Both Jacob and the God he serves viscerally engage their relationships and go to great lengths, including relying on others, to bring them to fruition.

At the heart of reflection upon atonement lies this question: What is the price for relationship, or, what is it that makes enduring relationships possible? Divine willingness to collaborate and innovate proves to be crucial. Divine desperation borne out of fear of loss draws out diverse strategies to salvage souls and set them in right relation. In order to reclaim and revive the various elements of the vineyard, God, in tandem with others, labors with might (verse 62). Enumerating the various measures taken to preserve an eternal relationship with each human individual, God emphasizes the ceaseless, collective efforts made on the vineyard's behalf: "I have nourished it, and I have digged about it, and I have pruned it, and I have dunged it; and I have stretched forth my hand all the day long" (verse 47). On the divine side, part of what is required is the ability and the willingness to see the latent potential for goodness, for thriving, in lives and locations where its realization seems impossible. Again and again, God instructs rather doubtful laborers to take actions that are counterintuitive and seemingly futile. Yet these measures bring God's purposes to fruition against human understanding. Often, these actions bring together dissimilar components that could prove to be adversarial to one another. Yet the fruitfulness that their integration yields demonstrates their innate need for interdependence. On the human side, then, the willingness to be intertwined and grafted together is required; the humility that accompanies this willingness prevents the "loftiness" that seeks to take strength to itself to the detriment of both self and others (verse 48).

Reverberating throughout Jacob's book, from making the Lamanites the teachers of Christian love and covenant, to allowing Sherem to give the final testimony of Christ, is the message that the wild branches are vital to the natural ones because they bring life (verse 34). Note that the Lamanites are typecast as wild in the Book of Mormon, including by Jacob's own son, Enos (Enos 1:20), and that Sherem is constructed equally as the quintessentially wild, given that he rebels against the highest religious authority of Nephite society and that his ethnic and religious identity are never definitively disclosed to us. We know nothing of his origins, and so he serves as the paradigmatic and undomesticated other. Through these means, Jacob demonstrates that Israel cannot survive or bring its covenant to culmination without others. Jacob learns that he too is dependent on the wild branches for the conversion of his people and the fulfillment of his ministry. Allowing wild branches to be grafted in, he cannot know at the outset whether this relationship will yield good fruit, and this ambiguity parallels God's experience in the allegory. After grafting the wild branches into the tame olive trees, God finds that good fruit grows again. The lord of the vineyard explains that "because of the much strength of the root thereof the wild branches have brought forth tame fruit. Now, if we had not grafted in these branches, the tree thereof would have perished" (Jacob 5:18). The wild branches need the strength of the natural tree's root to bear fruit, just as the natural tree needs the new life provided by the wild branches. In reality, the strength of the root is the humility and meekness to recognize that it cannot fulfill its potential independently. Only by bringing these disparate parts into right relation can both survive and flourish, rather than die as separate, closed-off systems.

True to form, Jacob turns assumptions about privilege on their head even in this arboreal context. While the tree in the enviable spot of the vineyard has withered (verse 43), the tree in the poor spot of ground has flourished. Observing the latter tree's abundant fruitfulness, the servant queries his master: "How comest thou hither to plant this tree, or this branch of the tree? For behold, it was the poorest spot in all the land of thy vineyard" (verse 21). Without hesitation, the lord of the vineyard replies: "Counsel me not; I knew that it was a poor spot of ground; wherefore, I said unto thee, I have nourished it this long time, and thou beholdest that it hath brought forth much fruit" (verse 22). ☞ Although the lord does not deny that some trees are asked to take root in circumstances that render them unduly vulnerable, he also avers that he offers personal attention and care to ensure that such trees are still capable of producing good fruit. Driving the point to its logical conclusion, the lord commands his servant to observe yet another tree that thrives in even poorer conditions: "behold I have planted another branch of the tree also; and thou knowest that this spot of ground was poorer than the first. But, behold the tree. I have nourished it this long time, and it hath brought forth much fruit; therefore, gather it, and lay it up against the season, that I may preserve it unto mine own self" (verse 23). Conversely, a tree nourished similarly but planted in a good spot of ground has only *partly* brought forth good fruit (verse 25). God is mindful of all so that divine love and care abound ubiquitously in creation. Yet, neither divine love nor other circumstances determine outcome. Even when love and care yield little response, God and Christ continue to innovate to coax good fruit out of each tree (verses 27–28).[8] These dauntless efforts are expended amid divine expressions of hopeful anticipation of regaining joy in the vineyard (verse 60) and lead God to call others to collaboratively "go to and labor with our might this last time" (verse 62). In this final effort, they "begin at the last that they may be first, and that the first may be last" (verse 63). Yet the realization of God's joy remains contingent upon the human response to God's efforts. Divine respect for human agency implies that in some instances God shares in the human situation of being able to do no more than remain in love as witness to alienation with uncertainty about the final outcome.

 I believe that Jacob identified with this particular tree, given that he was born in affliction in the wilderness. Despite adverse circumstances, he knows the tree can bear good fruit and be protected.

In Jacob's analysis, God's joy is realized along with God's purpose for the vineyard only because the various trees "became like unto one body; and the fruits were equal" (Jacob 5:74). In the vineyard's converted state, the lord is finally able to preserve the natural fruit, "which was most precious unto him from the beginning" (verse 74). It is in this state of unity and equality that the "Lord of the vineyard saw that his fruit was good, and that his vineyard was no more corrupt" (verse 75). By remaining a loving witness amid the ambiguity of human agency and an indeterminate future, divine love is brought to consummation through human responsiveness and reciprocity, which materializes in part through the formation of new, right relations among human beings. Jacob is uniquely able to envision this possibility because, although he is of Israel—and the namesake of the father of the twelve tribes—he identifies with wildness and knows its efficacy, so he can see the inherent goodness and necessity of those who might otherwise be discounted. Envisaging God as one who endures uncertainty with regard to God's own creation by remaining in loving relation to it informs and inspires Jacob's vocation as witness, as one who lovingly remains with his people, even in the face of ambiguity.

6

Final Thoughts

parting words

As he closes his record, Jacob re-emphasizes that his book has been necessarily brief, indicating that his "writing has been small" (Jacob 7:27). As we have seen, however, his space-limited record proves to be theologically dense. Prior to commending his son Enos, who will obediently care for the plates in his stead, to the reader, Jacob slips back into his baseline melancholy, perhaps out of sheer exhaustion from the spiritual and emotional energy he has expended in order to give us his prophetic text. Jacob assures his readers that he has written to the best of his knowledge and then observes that "the time passed away with us, and also our lives passed away like as it were unto us a dream, we being a lonesome and a solemn people, wanderers cast out from Jerusalem, born in tribulation in a *wild* wilderness (see FIGURE 1), and hated of our brethren, which caused wars and contentions; wherefore we did mourn out our days."[1] Here, Jacob speaks to the unpredictability and turbulence he and his people have endured, especially the solitary nature of their experience. Not only he and his younger brother but also his older siblings' children had been born in the wilderness (1 Ne. 17:1), ☞

☞ In describing the women in their company as bearing children in the wilderness, Nephi uses the word *wilderness* three times in a single verse.

110

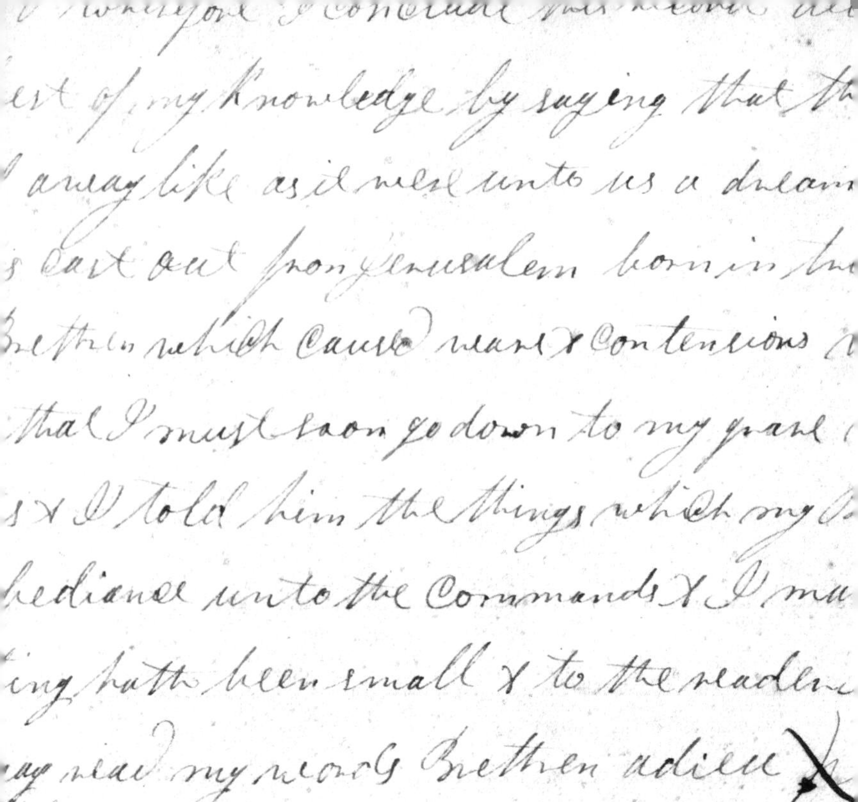

FIGURE 1 Page 110 of the original manuscript of the Book of Mormon uses the phrase "wild wilderness" (see the upper right side of the image); modern printings only use "wilderness." This image shows the end of the Book of Jacob and the begining of the Book of Enos (Jacob 7:26–27 and Enos 1:1–3). © Intellectual Reserve, Inc.

... passed away with us & also our lives ...

being a lonesome & a sollum People near ...

tion in a wild wilderness & hated of o...

... we did mourn out our days & I Jaco...

... you I said unto my son Enos take thee...

Nephi had commanded me & he prom...

of my writing upon thee plates which...

I farewell hopeing that many of my Br...

The Book of Enos Chapter...

my father that he was a just man ...

nurture & admonition of the Lord & bl...

... you of the wrestle which I had...

... my sins behold I went to hunt ...

... heard my father speak concer...

and their original liminality informs their identity and experience throughout their lives.

In the final reflections on his and his people's lives, Jacob laments the two major schisms they have suffered thus far: separation from the Jews and the abandonment of their homeland, Jerusalem, and their separation from their brethren, the Lamanites. These traumatic separations from their kin, which many experienced or perceived as forced upon them, seem to have made conscious engagement with the world nearly impossible. Jacob articulates that they collectively live in a dream state, implying that they exist in a mass dissociation, or a dreamlike trance that distances people from a reality that would otherwise be too overwhelming to cope with, which is indicative of traumatic stress lived out on a grand scale. This sense is amplified by the overarching theme of passivity in his description of Nephite life: every verb but one appears in the passive voice—life *happens to* the Nephites; they do not initiate actions themselves. They are "cast out," "born in tribulation," and "hated of" the Lamanites, and it is the hate that is directed toward the Nephites by the Lamanites that "caused wars and contentions" (verse 26). The Nephites suffer at the hands of other people and occurrences that they cannot control, or presumably even anticipate. The single thing that they do actively is to mourn out their days. It is strikingly ironic that one who made waking up his society a central feature of his ministry (Jacob 3:11), and who invited his people to rejoice in the reality of human agency (2 Ne. 10:23), closes his record in this soporific, passive tone. In the context of a life characterized by loss, ambiguity, and separation, Jacob's closing witness is less about triumph and certainty and more about choosing to remain a witness amid devastation and doubt. For Jacob, abjection has borne such totalizing effects on his life that it assumes a surreal quality.

His sense of dissociation appears to be exacerbated by the fact that his efforts to establish reconciliation and right relation among the Nephites and with the Lamanites have been frustrated; his poignant words speak to the sense of isolation that pervades his people's existence. From the first mention of Jacob to his final farewell, Jacob's life is characterized by a complex set of wrong relations and adverse situations that remain largely uncorrected despite all his efforts. Although Jacob has labored to help his people see themselves as essentially social beings who are implicated in one another's sins and sufferings, and to encourage them to embrace Christ with hope, he ends his life with a sense of solitariness and defeat. Even so, he *still* remains *with* his people and lays his life *before* God. In so doing, he offers "a picture not of victorious new life but of persistent witness to love's survival."[2] Regardless of how melancholy or despairing he may feel, or how little meaning he can make of his own life, his empathy with his people's sufferings and his love for God remain unmistakable. Amid the indefiniteness of his life's final meaning, Jacob has no choice but to surrender it—to offer it up.

Jacob's offering is summed up in the curious final word of the book: "adieu" (Jacob 7:27). This French word connotes a *last* farewell, indicating that one is making one's final departure. Further, *adieu* can be employed to express regret over a loss or in recognition that something will no longer be experienced. Etymologically, *adieu* comes from two words meaning "to God," and older versions of this phrase variously meant "go to God," "be commended to God," and "remain with God."[3] With this word choice, Jacob both conveys his final orientation to God and leaves his readers with a final invitation to similarly adopt or maintain this right relation. He further gets across the fragility of love that is ultimately expressed in its handing over. This "love that remains, that persists, that survives is neither triumphant nor...conquering....It is love that survives a death."[4] *Adieu* captures a life that remains equivocal and the loving witness that abides. Jacob finishes his role in the Book of Mormon just as he starts it, with consecration.

This ending is unique to Jacob among the Book of Mormon authors—it is the only instance of the word *adieu* in the English version of the scriptures—and it cannot be overlooked that his farewell bears Sherem's influence. Earlier in the chapter, Sherem concludes his confession of Christ with this statement: "I greatly fear lest my case shall be awful; but I confess unto God" (Jacob 7:19). Sherem utters these words with his dying breath. Uncertain about his divinely determined destination or what his dying profession of faith will amount to, Sherem leaves both to God. Jacob also expresses uncertainty about the final fate of his testament: "to the reader I bid farewell, *hoping* that many of my brethren may read my words. Brethren, adieu" (verse 27, emphasis added). Although Jacob expresses hope whereas Sherem expresses hopelessness, both admit that their concluding confessions share a degree of indeterminacy: Sherem cannot know if his testimony will be enough to secure a desirable state in the afterlife, just as Jacob is unsure if his fellow Nephites and later readers will make his words, and the consecrated sufferings that inform them, efficacious by conforming their lives to the truth he unfolds for them. Amid this ambiguity, both lay their words and their lives before God. Sherem makes plain that while other human beings can hear his words, he confesses "unto God." Taking Jacob's last word as an aspiration heightens the parallel—God continues to be his goal, not one he asserts he has attained, and he inspires his people, even with his last breath, to make this eternal relation their objective as well. Jacob, no less than Sherem, lacks the ability to ensure that his testimony will change the fate of the Nephites. Although he—rather uncharacteristically—does not communicate any anxiety with regard to his state in the afterlife, he still realizes that for all of his painstaking efforts to give his people and later readers a vision of godly, faithful society as part and parcel to his witness of Christ, his life's labor and ministry rest finally in the hands of God, no less than does Sherem's fate. Jacob, just like anyone and everyone else, is left only to hope.

hope

Coming full circle, it is useful to realize that what is perhaps most fascinating about Jacob's incitement to view Christ's death and suffer his cross is, of course, the fact that the death of Christ has not yet transpired when he writes his record. What does it mean to be inspired by beholding Gethsemane and the cross, and to suffer that cross, when there is as yet nothing to behold? On this point, Jacob both exhibits and induces what one scholar dubs "radical hope." He explains, "What makes this hope radical is that it is directed toward a future goodness that transcends the current ability to understand what it is. Radical hope anticipates a good for which those who have the hope as yet lack the appropriate concepts with which to understand it."[5] While this concept certainly seems to be at play in pre-Christian discussions of atonement in the Book of Mormon, Jacob seems to want his people to move from radical hope to something less nebulous and more fleshed out. Jacob describes this hope not in terms of radicality but in terms of goodness.

Jacob's wish for his people is that subsequent to their resurrection, they may be worthy to be presented as the "first fruits of Christ unto God," which would require them to have "faith, and to have obtained a good hope of glory in him before he manifesteth himself in the flesh" (Jacob 4:11). Jacob wants them to obtain not just hope, but a *good* hope. Presumably, by "a good hope" he means a substantive and specific hope, one that is based upon a knowledge of and relationship with Christ that is possible even prior to his earthly ministry. Jacob presents his people with the task of establishing a more concrete and defined hope by viewing Christ's death and suffering Christ's cross prior to the relevant events transpiring in history. In one sense, Jacob is asking his audience not so much to know about Christ as to *know* Christ. A good hope is based not on apprehension of historical facts but on an appreciation of who Christ most essentially is, one who empties himself in order to make eternal relationship possible with everyone who desires it. A person must intimately come to know Christ's character and how he relates to her individually; this can create trust in his unfailing efforts on behalf of her personal salvation (see Jacob 7:25).

While many pre-Christian prophets gesture in fruitful directions in their discussions of Christ and the atonement, the context in which Jacob writes seems unique and illuminates an especially useful feature of these exercises in Christian imagination. Perhaps Jacob focuses on the theme of hope because he has in mind a society rife with disempowered persons, a plight with which he has been able to identify in various ways for much of his life. For those whose agency has been compromised and are suffering as a result of others' sins, hope presents itself as a particular kind of agency. Because it is based upon an *internal* envisioning that leads to personal relationship with Christ, hope can be enacted even when unjust social structures create a context of compromised agency. For Jacob, who regards human beings as lowly and "of the dust," hope is critical because it summons the divine grace that empowers one to accomplish great things despite one's weakness (Jacob 4:7). One lesson to be gleaned from the pre-Christian prophets of the Book of Mormon in general, and perhaps Jacob in particular, is that one's hope in and relationship to Christ is determined neither by one's external circumstances and place in society nor by Christ himself. Regardless of the era of history one is born into, or the place in the vineyard that one occupies, one can create a relationship with Christ through hopeful envisaging. It is through personal desire, more than any other variable, that one determines both the degree and content of one's spiritual knowledge (verse 14). That is, the fruit of our lives and our conformity to Christ is finally left not to coincidence but to our continual efforts to see him and suffer with him, and to do so with hope. Of course, what we must take away from the book of Jacob, if nothing else, is a deep sense that this hope in Christ must also impel us to hopefully re-envision human communities in ways that are more just, charitable, and faithful, and to labor with longsuffering to convert these visions into our reality.

Conclusion

In his relatively short book, Jacob both typifies and testifies of Christ. He invites all people to view the death of Christ and, I believe, to view every aspect of reality through the lens of reconciliation that it affords. In this way, we are reminded of God's infinite and ever available love, which ceaselessly strives to meet each individual in her extremity. This love does not just desire our purity and worthiness of salvation, although it certainly both desires our conversion and makes it possible. This love shows us the way through to flourishing and fruitfulness, reminding us that all objectives worth seeking ultimately rely upon faithful communities who strive to reach back in love toward the divine for their attainment. This communal and faithful love requires us to see all human beings as equals, a vision that is facilitated by viewing one another through the lens of the death of Christ: we are all equally in need of reconciliation to God and all equally loved by both God and Christ, a truth attested by Christ's willingness to suffer and make the atonement equally available to all. Atonement will not override human agency, but it is always before us, beckoning us to envision ourselves and one another with a profound hope through the loving eyes of the Christ on the cross. With these truths in mind, we can empty ourselves of pride in the face of other human beings, recognizing that we can learn how to be more faithful from anyone, even those we would otherwise misjudge as faithless. Appreciating that life is full of ambiguity, and that often human existence, even for the faithful, is characterized by the uncertainty and sorrow of Holy Saturday rather than the reassurance and rejoicing of

Easter Sunday, we come to embrace what it means to remain with Christ, as loving witnesses of him even as we are unsure of what the future holds. The ambiguous nature of our lives, then, need not culminate in ambivalence; instead, this ambiguity can engender in us, as it did for Jacob, and for the God that he reveals to us, a passionate entanglement with the world when we understand that our religion is realized through our relationships and our salvation is inseparable from the structuring of our societies.

Further Reading

Green, Deidre Nicole. "Prolepsis in the Past Tense: The Anachronistic Atonement of Abinadite Prophecy." In *God Himself Shall Come Down: Reading Mosiah 15,* edited by Andrew Smith and Joseph M. Spencer. Seattle, WA: Latter-day Saint Theology Seminar, 2020. Focusing on Abinadi, I examine why pre-Christian prophets speak about atonement as occurring both in the past and in the future. The concept of *kenosis* from Philippians 2 likewise frames this discussion.

Hilton, John, III. "Jacob's Textual Legacy." *Journal of the Book of Mormon and Other Restoration Scripture* 22, no. 2 (2013): 52–65. Hilton demonstrates the influence of Jacob's ministry on other Book of Mormon prophets.

Kierkegaard, Søren. *Works of Love.* Edited and translated by Howard V. Hong and Edna H. Hong. Princeton, NJ: Princeton University Press, 1995. Nineteenth-century writer Søren Kierkegaard reflects on the commandment to love the neighbor. His views on love resonate with Jacob's and inform my reading.

Miller, Adam S., and Joseph M. Spencer, eds. *Christ and Antichrist: Reading Jacob 7.* Provo, UT: Neal A. Maxwell Institute for Religious Scholarship, 2017. This anthology covers an array of perspectives on Jacob 7, based on close readings.

Webb, Jenny. "Death, Time, and Redemption: Structural Possibilities and Thematic Potential in Jacob 7:26." *Journal of Book of Mormon Studies* 24, no. 1 (2015): 231–37. Webb explores the structure and themes in Jacob 7:26, focusing on the relational schisms that cause Jacob's mourning and the hope that the possibility of healing offers.

Endnotes

SERIES INTRODUCTION

1. Elder Neal A. Maxwell, "The Children of Christ," university devotional, Brigham Young University, Provo, UT, 4 February 1990, https://speeches.byu.edu/talks/neal-a-maxwell_children-christ/.

2. Elder Neal A. Maxwell, "The Inexhaustible Gospel," university devotional, Brigham Young University, Provo, UT, 18 August 1992, https://speeches.byu.edu/talks/neal-a-maxwell/inexhaustible-gospel/.

3. Elder Neal A. Maxwell, "The Book of Mormon: A Great Answer to 'The Great Question,'" address, Book of Mormon Symposium, Brigham Young University, Provo, UT, 10 October 1986, reprinted in *The Voice of My Servants: Apostolic Messages on Teaching, Learning, and Scripture,* ed. Scott C. Esplin and Richard Neitzel Holzapfel (Provo, UT: Religious Studies Center, Brigham Young University; Salt Lake City: Deseret Book, 2010), 221–38, https://rsc.byu.edu/archived/voice-my-servants/book-mormon-great-answer-great-question.

1

1. Royal Skousen, ed., "Jacob 7:26," in *Analysis of Textual Variants of the Book of Mormon: The Earliest Text, Part 2: 2 Nephi 11–Mosiah 16,* Critical Text of the Book of Mormon 4 (Provo, UT: Foundation for Ancient Research and Mormon Studies, 2014), 1069–70; also available at https://interpreterfoundation.org/books/atv/p2/.

2. G. Johannes Botterweck, Helmer Ringgren, and Heinz-Josef Fabry, eds., *Theological Dictionary of the Old Testament,* (Grand Rapids, MI: Eerdmans, 1999), s.v. "midbar," 8:91.

3. Jacob Rennaker, "Divine Dream Time: The Hope and Hazard of Revelation," in *Christ and Antichrist: Reading Jacob 7*, ed. Adam S. Miller and Joseph M. Spencer (Provo, UT: Neal A. Maxwell Institute for Religious Scholarship, 2017), 52.

4. I thank Kylie Turley for this suggestion.

5. See *American Dictionary of the English Language*, 1st ed. (1828), s.v. "affliction," http://webstersdictionary1828.com/Dictionary/affliction. See also *American Dictionary of the English Language*, s.v. "rudeness," http://webstersdictionary1828.com/Dictionary/rudeness.

6. Matthew L. Bowen, "Jacob's Protector," *Interpreter: A Journal of Mormon Scripture 27* (Orem, UT: Interpreter Foundation, 2017): 235–37.

7. David A. Bednar, "Meek and Lowly of Heart," April 2018 general conference of The Church of Jesus Christ of Latter-day Saints, https://www.churchofjesuschrist.org/study/general-conference/2018/04/meek-and-lowly-of-heart?lang=eng.

2

1. *American Dictionary of the English Language*, 1st ed. (1828), s.v. "consecrated," http://webstersdictionary1828.com/Dictionary/consecrated.

2. *Oxford English Dictionary,* s.v. "consecrate," accessed June 3, 2019, https://www-oed-com.erl.lib.byu.edu/view/Entry/39491?.

3. I acknowledge George Handley for this insight.

4. *American Dictionary of the English Language*, 1st ed. (1828), s.v. "view," http://webstersdictionary1828.com/Dictionary/view.

5. *American Dictionary of the English Language,* s.v. "view."

6. Brian Gregor, *A Philosophical Anthropology of the Cross: The Cruciform Self* (Bloomington: Indiana University Press, 2013), 16.

7. Shelly Rambo, *Spirit and Trauma: A Theology of Remaining* (Louisville, KY: Westminster John Knox Press, 2010), 131, 109, 132–35.

8. I acknowledge Sydney Squires for this observation.

3

1. Sin is first described as a social phenomenon when Nephi quotes Isaiah (2 Ne. 24:21). Nephi does not elaborate on this idea, and it is not clearly articulated by Lehi either.

2. Søren Kierkegaard, *Christian Discourses,* ed. and trans. Howard V. Hong and Edna H. Hong (Princeton, NJ: Princeton University Press, 1997), 246.

3. Ingolf U. Dalferth, *Creatures of Possibility: The Theological Basis of Human Freedom,* trans. Jo Bennett (Grand Rapids, MI: Baker Academic, 2016), 197; originally published as *Umsonst: Eine Erinnerung an Die Kreative Passivitat Des Menschen* (Tübingen: Mohr, 2011).

4. Jared Hickman, "The Book of Mormon as Amerindian Apocalypse," *American Literature 86,* no. 3 (Durham, NC: Duke University Press, 2014), 452.

5. Kimberly Berkey notes that Jacob's question, What am I? rather than the question, Who am I? suggests that Jacob "takes on an abject, creaturely posture." Kimberly M. Berkey, "The Lord's Prayer(s) in Jacob 7," in Miller and Spencer, eds., *Christ and Antichrist: Reading Jacob 7,* 32.

6. Terry Warner states that "Sherem's was an aggravated case of living a lie." C. Terry Warner, "Jacob," in Arthur R. Bassett et al., *The Book of Mormon: It Begins with a Family* (Salt Lake City, UT: Deseret Book, 1983), 51.

7. Sherem shares a common trait with Nehor and Korihor: he is compelled by the power of God to be humble, rather than choosing to humble himself (see Alma 32:14). Instead of voluntarily shedding beliefs he knows to be false, God forces them out of him. While his words are true and accomplish good for others, their potential to fully convert Sherem into a new being is mitigated because they are compelled.

4

1. Kimberly Berkey helpfully describes the "Lehitic covenant" as "encompass[ing] all the prophecies concerning Lehi's posterity," including "four basic elements: (1) settlement in a promised land (2 Ne. 1:5); (2) the familiar assurance that 'Inasmuch as ye shall keep my commandments ye shall prosper in the land' (Jarom 1:9); (3) a guarantee that Lehi's seed will never perish (2 Ne. 25:21); and (4) the promise that a record will come forth to bring the remnant of Lehi's seed to the knowledge of the covenant." Kimberly M. Berkey, "Works of Darkness: Secret Combinations and Covenant Displacement in the Book of Mormon," in *Reading Nephi Reading Isaiah: Reading 2 Nephi 26–27,* 2nd edition, ed. Joseph M. Spencer and Jenny Webb (Provo, UT: Neal A. Maxwell Institute for Religious Scholarship, 2016), 105–6.

2. For a similar argument, see Joseph Spencer's volume on the book of 1 Nephi in this series. Joseph M. Spencer, *1st Nephi: a brief theological introduction* (Provo, UT: Neal A. Maxwell Institute for Religious Scholarship, 2020), 100–104.

3. Joseph Smith History, vol. A–1 [23 December 1805–30 August 1834], 6, The Joseph Smith Papers, http:// www.josephsmithpapers.org/paper-summary/ history-1838-1856-volume-a-1-23-december-1805-30-august-1834/6.

4. I acknowledge Rosalynde Welch, whose interpretation of Ether helped me to recognize similarities between Moroni and Jacob's perspectives on weakness. See her volume in this series.

5. Alma 1:30 describes the communal sharing that Jacob envisions: "in their prosperous circumstances, they did not send away any who were naked, or that were hungry, or that were athirst, or that were sick, or that had not been nourished; and they did not set their hearts upon riches; therefore they were liberal to all, both old and young, both bond and free, both male and female, whether out of the church or in the church, having no respect to persons as to those who stood in need."

6. I acknowledge Anthea D. Butler for her insight on this section.

7. See W. Paul Reeve, *Religion of a Different Color: Race and the Mormon Struggle for Whiteness* (New York: Oxford University Press, 2015).

8. Barbara A. Holmes, *Race and the Cosmos: An Invitation to View the World Differently* (Harrisburg, PA: Trinity Press International, 2002), xvi, 103.

9. See Max Perry Mueller, *Race and the Making of the Mormon People* (Chapel Hill: University of North Carolina Press, 2017).

10. Marvin Perkins, "Blacks and the Priesthood" (fireside presentation, Los Angeles, CA, 8 September 2002), https://www.fairmormon. org/archive/publications/blacks-and-the-priesthood.

11. Jacob's jarring language ought to awaken modern readers to the realization of how unacceptable more insidious forms of supremacy are. His language may also indicate that Jacob is both critical of and constrained by the culture and language in which his ministry is embedded. Book of Mormon authors explicitly identified their own witnesses as limited and enjoined contemporary readers to "give thanks unto God" for making their "imperfections" known so that contemporary readers might "learn to be more wise than we have been" (Mormon 9:31). From Jacob's struggle to challenge false ideas in language that may seem to reinforce them, we can learn how

finite our conceptions of reality are and how much we need various perspectives to help us make our societies as godly as they can possibly be.

12. *Oxford English Dictionary*, s.v. "gross," https://www.oed.com/view/Entry/81765?result=4&rskey=M8UUei&.

13. *American Dictionary of the English Language*, 1st ed. (1828), s.v. "gross," http://webstersdictionary1828.com/Dictionary/gross.

14. *Oxford English Dictionary*, s.v. "iniquity," https://www.oed.com/view/Entry/96048?redirectedFrom=iniquity&.

15. Maren Johnson, "Harden Not Our Hearts: The Opposite of a Hard Heart Is Not Soft," (unpublished manuscript, 29 December 2017), 5, https://scholarsarchive.byu.edu/english_symposium/2018/mormon/2/.

5

1. *American Dictionary of the English Language*, 1st ed. (1828), s.v. "cleave," http://webstersdictionary1828.com/Dictionary/cleave.

2. Jacob introduces the term "infinite atonement" to the Book of Mormon both sequentially and in the timeline of the narrative, not in terms of dictation order in the translation process.

3. Jacob's analysis of the atonement as it applies to agents *in extremis* means that the Book of Mormon cannot be reduced to a text addressing the theological debates of the nineteenth century, although it does that; it is a book that also anticipates the major religious challenge of the latter half of the twentieth century, which continues to challenge us in the twenty-first century, namely, How does one understand God, divine goodness, and human redemption in the face of massive suffering caused intentionally by human beings? What is the meaning of atonement in the wake of ethnic cleansing, of the brutalization and annihilation of those once considered neighbors and kin? The Book of Mormon positions itself to answer these questions and Jacob's empathy attunes him to these issues in particular. Jacob's preoccupation with the fact that all sins begin with thoughts stems from his understanding of how devastating and deadly their thought-sins will prove to be and why the atonement must operate on us at the level of thought.

4. Elder Jeffrey R. Holland asserts that the allegory is primarily about atonement: "From all the distant places of sin and alienation in which the children of the Father find themselves, it has always been the work of Christ (and his disciples) in every dispensation to gather them, heal

them, and unite them with their Master." Jeffrey R. Holland, *Christ and the New Covenant* (Salt Lake City, UT: Deseret Book, 1997), 166.

5. I gratefully acknowledge conversations with Benjamin Keogh for helping me articulate atonement in this way.

6. Catherine Keller, *Face of the Deep: A Theology of Becoming* (New York: Routledge, 2003), 233.

7. Rambo, *Spirit and Trauma,* 130–31. Note that Rambo is drawing on Keller to strengthen her own notion of middle Spirit.

8. To salvage yet another tree that despite its choice location failed to produce fruit, God instructs the servant and laborers to draw branches from the nethermost part of the vineyard (verse 52). That is, those that are figuratively the furthest away hold forth the possibility of introducing enough newness to save the trees, which cannot survive on their own.

6

1. Skousen, "Jacob 7:26," in *Analysis of Textual Variants of the Book of Mormon: The Earliest Text, Part 2: 2 Nephi 11–Mosiah 16*, 1069–70; also available at https://interpreterfoundation.org/books/atv/p2/. Emphasis added.

2. Rambo, *Spirit and Trauma,* 110.

3. *Oxford English Dictionary,* s.v. "adieu," https://www.oed.com/view/Entry/2374?result=2&rskey=qocVfp&.

4. Rambo, *Spirit and Trauma,* 137.

5. Jonathan Lear, *Radical Hope: Ethics in the Face of Cultural Devastation* (Cambridge, MA: Harvard University Press, 2008), 103.

Editions of the
Book of Mormon

Most Latter-day Saints are familiar principally with the official
edition of the Book of Mormon published in 2013 by The Church of
Jesus Christ of Latter-day Saints. It contains the canonical text of the
book, divided into chapters of relatively even length with numbered
verses for ease of access. Its footnotes aim to assist readers in seeking doctrinal understanding.

Other Book of Mormon editions are available and often helpful.
Among these are official editions from earlier in the scripture's pub-
lishing history, which are relatively accessible. There are also editions published recently by a variety of presses meant to make the
text more readable. Both types of editions are referred to throughout
Book of Mormon: brief theological introductions. Also of importance
(and occasionally referred to) are the manuscript sources for the
printed editions of the Book of Mormon.

manuscript sources

Unfortunately, the original manuscript of the Book of Mormon was
damaged during the nineteenth century, but substantial portions
of it remain. All known extant portions have been published in
typescript in Royal Skousen, ed., *The Original Manuscript of the Book
of Mormon: Typographical Facsimile of the Extant Text* (Provo, UT:
Foundation for Ancient Research and Mormon Studies (FARMS),
2001). A future volume of the Joseph Smith Papers will publish
images of the extant manuscript, along with a typescript.

After completing the original manuscript's dictation, Joseph
Smith assigned Oliver Cowdery to produce a second manuscript
copy of the text. That manuscript has been called the printer's
manuscript since it was designed for use by the first printer of the
Book of Mormon. The printer's manuscript, which is more or less
entirely intact, also contains corrections and other editorial mark-
ings inserted when the second (1837) edition of the Book of Mormon
was being prepared. A typescript of the printer's manuscript can be
found in Royal Skousen, ed., *The Printer's Manuscript of the Book of
Mormon: Typographical Facsimile of the Entire Text in Two Parts,*

2 vols. (Provo, UT: FARMS, 2001). Full color images of the manuscript were subsequently published along with a transcript in the Joseph Smith Papers series: Royal Skousen and Robin Scott Jensen, eds., *Printer's Manuscript of the Book of Mormon*, 2 vols., vol. 3 of the *Revelations and Translations* series of The Joseph Smith Papers, ed. Dean C. Jessee, Ronald K. Esplin, and Richard Lyman Bushman (Salt Lake City: Church Historian's Press, 2015). The images and transcript of the printer's manuscript are also available at the Joseph Smith Papers website (www.josephsmithpapers.org/the-papers/ revelations-and-translations/jsppr3).

historical editions

Multiple editions of the Book of Mormon were published during the lifetime of Joseph Smith. The first edition, published in Palmyra, New York, in 1830, appeared without versification and with fewer chapter divisions than the present canonical text (see FIGURE 2). The text of the 1830 edition is available electronically at the Joseph Smith Papers website (www.josephsmithpapers.org/the-papers/revelations-and-translations/jsppr4) and in print through various publishers as a replica edition. The 1830 text is also available in Robert A. Rees and Eugene England, eds., *The Reader's Book of Mormon* (Salt Lake City, UT: Signature Books, 2008), which is divided into seven pocket-sized volumes (each with an introduction by a scholar).

Joseph Smith introduced numerous minor changes into the text of the Book of Mormon when it was prepared for a second edition in 1837. Many of these changes are marked in the printer's manuscript. Most were aimed at correcting grammatical issues, but some, in a small handful of cases, were also aimed at clarifying the meaning of the text or its doctrinal implications. The 1837 edition is available electronically at the Joseph Smith Papers website (www.josephsmithpapers.org/the-papers/revelations-and-translations/jsppr4).

A third edition was prepared under Joseph Smith's direction in 1840, and evidence makes clear that the original manuscript was consulted carefully in preparing this edition. Some important errors in the earlier editions were corrected, further grammatical improvements were introduced, and a few other changes were made to the text for purposes of clarification. The 1840 edition can be read at the Joseph Smith Papers website (www.josephsmithpapers.org /the-papers/revelations-and-translations/jsppr4). It forms the basis for at least one printed edition as well: *The Book of Mormon*, trans. Joseph Smith Jr. (New York: Penguin Books, 2008), which contains

THE

BOOK OF MORMON:

AN ACCOUNT WRITTEN BY THE HAND OF MOR-
MON, UPON PLATES TAKEN FROM
THE PLATES OF NEPHI.

Wherefore it is an abridgment of the Record of the People of Nephi; and also of the Lamanites; written to the Lamanites, which are a remnant of the House of Israel; and also to Jew and Gentile; written by way of commandment, and also by the spirit of Prophesy and of Revelation. Written, and sealed up, and hid up unto the LORD, that they might not be destroyed; to come forth by the gift and power of GOD unto the interpretation thereof; sealed by the hand of Moroni, and hid up unto the LORD, to come forth in due time by the way of Gentile; the interpretation thereof by the gift of GOD; an abridgment taken from the Book of Ether.

Also, which is a Record of the People of Jared, which were scattered at the time the LORD confounded the language of the people when they were building a tower to get to Heaven: which is to shew unto the remnant of the House of Israel how great things the LORD hath done for their fathers; and that they may know the covenants of the LORD, that they are not cast off forever; and also to the convincing of the Jew and Gentile that JESUS is the CHRIST, the ETERNAL GOD, manifesting Himself unto all nations. And now if there be fault, it be the mistake of men; wherefore condemn not the things of GOD, that ye may be found spotless at the judgment seat of CHRIST.

BY JOSEPH SMITH, JUNIOR,

AUTHOR AND PROPRIETOR.

PALMYRA:

PRINTED BY E. B. GRANDIN, FOR THE AUTHOR.

1830.

FIGURE 2 The title page of the original 1830 edition of The Book of Mormon. © Intellectual Reserve, Inc.

a helpful introduction by Laurie Maffly-Kipp, a scholar of American religious history.

One other edition of the Book of Mormon appeared during the lifetime of Joseph Smith—an 1841 British edition, which was largely based on the 1837 edition and therefore lacked corrections and other improvements that appear in the 1840 edition. It, too, is available electronically at the Joseph Smith Papers website (www.josephsmithpapers.org/the-papers/revelations-and-translations/jsppr4).

In 1879, Latter-day Saint apostle Orson Pratt completed one of the more influential editions of the Book of Mormon published after Joseph Smith's death. Pratt lamented that too many Latter-day Saints left the scripture unread on the shelf. He sought to create an easier reading experience by dividing up the originally long chapters and adding verse numbers—revisions which have largely remained unchanged in the Church's official edition to the present. He also pioneered a system of cross-references and other explanatory footnotes. Most of Pratt's notes were removed or replaced in subsequent official editions—most thoroughly in the Church's 1981 edition when new descriptive chapter headings were introduced. These headings can still be found, with a few minor updates, in the 2013 edition.

A detailed and helpful devotional treatment of the publication history of the Book of Mormon can be found in Richard E. Turley Jr. and William W. Slaughter, *How We Got the Book of Mormon* (Salt Lake City, UT: Deseret Book, 2011). These authors trace developments in the format and study apparatuses used to present the text of the Book of Mormon to audiences from the 1850s to the present.

study and reading editions

The most important scholarly editions of the Book of Mormon are Grant Hardy, ed., *The Book of Mormon: A Reader's Edition* (Urbana and Chicago: University of Illinois Press, 2003); and Royal Skousen, ed., *The Book of Mormon: The Earliest Text* (New Haven, CT: Yale University Press, 2009).

Hardy's edition repackages the text of the 1921 public domain edition of the Book of Mormon. It contains a helpful introduction, a series of useful appendices, and a straightforward presentation of the text in a highly readable format. Footnotes are minimal—they are used only to clarify direct references or allusions within the text, to track dates, or to alert readers about original chapter divisions. This edition contains modern chapter and verse divisions, but they are unobtrusively typeset. The text is presented in straightforward paragraphs, with one-line headings marking text divisions. Poetry is set off in poetic lines, as in modern editions of the Bible.

Skousen's edition is the result of his quarter-century-long work with the manuscript and printed sources for the Book of Mormon text. The edition aims to reproduce as closely as can be reconstructed the words originally dictated by Joseph Smith to his scribes. Chapter and verse divisions familiar from recent editions are in the text (and symbols mark original chapter breaks), but the text is presented in what Skousen calls "sense lines"—each line containing (on Skousen's reconstruction) approximately what the prophet would have dictated at one time before pausing to allow his scribe to write. The edition contains helpful introductory material and a summary appendix noting significant differences between *The Earliest Text* and the current official edition. It is otherwise without any apparatus for the reader.

The most significant edition of the Book of Mormon deliberately constructed for a lay reading audience is Grant Hardy, ed., *The Book of Mormon: Another Testament of Jesus Christ,* Maxwell Institute Study Edition (Salt Lake City and Provo, UT: Neal A. Maxwell Institute for Religious Studies, Deseret Book, and BYU Religious Studies Center, 2018). In this edition, Hardy uses the text of the 2013 official edition of the Book of Mormon but presents it in a readable way for everyday students of the volume. This edition reproduces the best of what appears in Hardy's *Reader's Edition* but adds further resources in the introductory and appendix materials. The footnotes are updated and expanded to include variant readings from the original and printer's manuscripts, and to provide notes about other textual details. The body of the text is presented, as in the *Reader's Edition*, in a straightforward fashion, readable and interrupted only by one-line headings. Modern chapter and verse divisions, as well as original chapter divisions, are easily visible.

Index

TOPICS

140

141

142

Colophon

The text of the book is typeset in Arnhem,
Fred Smeijer's 21st-century-take on late
18th-century Enlightenment-era letterforms
known for their sturdy legibility and clarity
of form. Captions and figures are typset in
Quaadraat Sans, also by Fred Smeijers.
The book title and chapter titles are typeset
in Thema by Nikola Djurek.

Printed on Domtar Lynx 74 gsm,
Forest Stewardship Council (FSC) Certified.

Printed by Brigham Young University Print & Mail Services

Woodcut illuminations **Brian Kershisnik**
Book design & typography **Douglas Thomas**
Production typesetting **Natalie Miles, Ruth Eldredge Thomas**

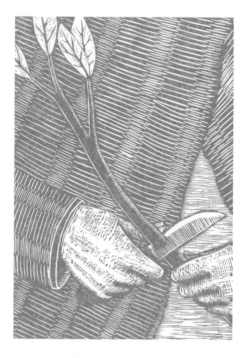

Jacob 5:4 And it came to pass that the master of the vineyard went forth, and he saw that his olive-tree began to decay; and he said: I will prune it, and dig about it, and nourish it, that perhaps it may shoot forth young and tender branches, and it perish not.